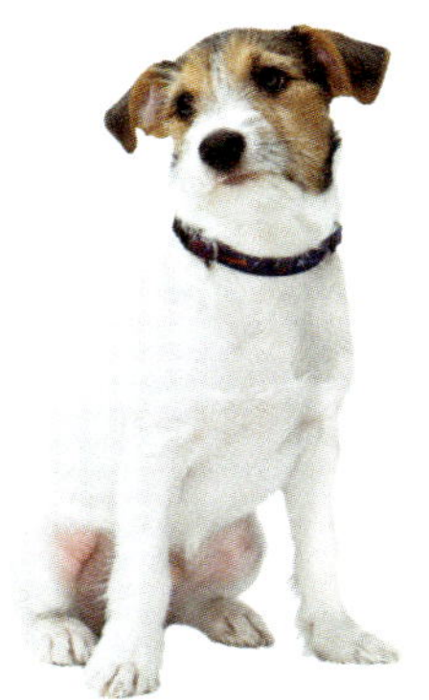

ArtBrands

wenn Hunde Beuys fressen
when dogs eat Beuys

eine Sammlung von · a collection by
Michael Klant

Inhalt | Contents

Mehr so nebenbei erzählte mir Michael Klant an einem sonnigen Herbstnachmittag des Jahres 2005 von seiner Sammlung. Von den mehr als 70 Stücken, die im Laufe der Jahre zusammengekommen waren und sich stetig vermehrten. Ich fand die Idee, nach Produkten mit Künstlernamen zu suchen, zwar witzig, wusste aber nichts weiter damit anzufangen. Mit Museum und Kunst hatte das ja eigentlich kaum etwas zu tun. Ein, wie ich fand, doch eher intellektualistisch-spielerisches Konsumpuzzle.

Ein Besuch, ganz unverbindlich, wurde vereinbart. Mit Neugier, schon, mehr aber auch nicht. Doch kaum standen sie vor mir, verteilt in seinem Atelier, die Zahnpastatube der Firma Rembrandt, die Espressotasse von Cellini, der Sack Hundefutter namens Beuys – und all die anderen aus dem Klant'schen Inventar, war ich der Verlockung auch schon erlegen: Was wäre, wenn man diese Ansammlung hochkarätiger Namen, diese merkwürdige Produktpalette ausstellte? Wenn sich das öffentlichkeitswirksame Versprechen, eine Sammlung aus Meisternamen der Kunstgeschichte vom Mittelalter bis zur Gegenwart erstmals zu zeigen, ganz anders erfüllte, als von den Besuchern erwartet?

Glaubwürdigkeit, Leichtsinn, Verführung, Ästhetik, Original, Spekulation, Wahrnehmung: Es gab kaum ein Thema zwischen Kunst und Kommerz, das wir nicht diskutierten. Bis wir feststellten, dass wir und alle, denen wir von dem Projekt erzählten, unsere Bedenken immer wieder lachend beiseite schoben. Wir hatten einfach Lust darauf, sie zu machen, diese Highlight-Ausstellung der anderen Art.

It was a sunny afternoon in the fall of 2005 when Michael Klant happened to mention his collection of more than 70 works that he had gathered over the years and continued to add to. While I found the idea of looking for products bearing the names of famous artists humorous in a way, it didn't strike a deeper chord, and I saw no connection between it and art or my personal work as the curator of a museum. I found it to be more of a playfully intellectual pursuit, like assembling a puzzle whose pieces—all of them consumer goods—had a surprising associative ring.

I nonetheless agreed to come and have a look. I was curious after all, but not more than curious. Within moments of my arrival that day, however, something unexpected happened. There I was . . . I had scarcely taken a look at the various items assembled in Klant's studio—the tube of Rembrandt toothpaste, the Cellini espresso cup, the bag of Beuys dog food, and all the other "works" in the Klantian inventory—when I suddenly found myself entertaining an irresistible thought. "What if?" I thought. "What if this collection of famous names, this unusual line of products was exhibited in a museum? What if the publicly issued promise to exhibit for the first time a collection of works bearing famous names from the history of art, ranging from the Middle Ages to the present, was kept in a manner that was completely different from what the museum's visitors expected?"

Credibility, frivolity, seduction, aesthetics, originality, speculation, and perception: there was hardly a subject at the confluence of art and commerce that we didn't discuss. Until we discovered that we—and everyone we talked to about the project—were left only to dismiss our reservations with a laugh. We simply wanted to realize the project, this exhibition of highlights of another kind.

ArtBrands treibt den Markenbonus auf die Spitze. Zeigt Exponate eines irregulären Wettbewerbs. Befreit den Museumsgänger von latenter Kleptomanie. Denn wer dieser Leidenschaft des Sammelns erliegt, sieht die Welt, die Warenwelt und die Kunstwelt, mit anderen Augen. Hat seinen Kandinsky als Schlüsselanhänger immer in der Tasche, der ihm die Türen zum Verständnis öffnet und schließt.

Ich danke allen, die mitgeholfen haben, diese Ausstellung zu verwirklichen. Allen voran Michael Klant für sein Vertrauen, seine Kollegialität und seine ansteckende Begeisterung. Ulrich Birtel, durch den die Ausstellung ihr unverwechselbares grafisches Gesicht bekam. Den Leihgebern, die ArtBrands um einige unerreichbar scheinende Stücke großzügig ergänzt haben. Den Autoren für ihre das Thema von verschiedenen Seiten so originell und fundiert beleuchtenden Texte. Annette Kulenkampff vom Hatje Cantz Verlag für ihr spontanes Interesse an dem geplanten Katalog. Dem Förderverein des Museums für Neue Kunst und allen Sponsoren, die uns die notwendige finanzielle Absicherung gaben. Besonders aber danke ich allen »beteiligten« Künstlern und Künstlerinnen. Ohne ihre wunderbaren Werke hätten wir diese abenteuerliche Reise nicht antreten können. ■

Jochen Ludwig

ArtBrands takes the notion of a brand bonus to extreme. It displays participants in an irregular competition. It liberates museum visitors from their latent kleptomania. For those who fall prey to this collector's passion will see the world, the world of commodities, and the world of art in an entirely new light. They will always have their Kandinsky—in the form of a keychain—in their pockets, giving them what they need to open and close the door to understanding.

I would like to thank all of those who helped to make this exhibition possible. My special thanks go out to Michael Klant for his trust, collegiality and contagious enthusiasm, Ulrich Birtel who was responsible for giving the exhibition its unmistakable graphical face, the donors who generously helped to expand the ArtBrands collection by providing a number of pieces that seemed unobtainable, the authors for their illuminating contributions, Annette Kulenkampff from Hatje Cantz Verlag for her spontaneous interest in helping to develop the exhibition catalogue, the Friends of The Freiburg Museum of New Art, and other sponsors who gave us the necessary financial support, and, last but not least, all of the "participating" artists without whose wonderful works we would never have been able to embark on this adventurous journey. ■

Jochen Ludwig

ArtBrands – ein Märchen aus der Warenwelt | ArtBrands —A Warehouse Fairy Tale

Ein Kaufladen am Niederrhein. Irgendwo zwischen Kalkar und Kleve. Flaches Land. Grenzgebiet. Ein paar einfache Regale, Kühltheke, ein Zeitschriftenständer, die Lotto-Annahmestelle. Es ist kurz vor Ladenschluss. Auf dem Heimweg von der Arbeit macht Franz Leenders schnell noch den Einkauf. Mittwochs übernimmt er den immer. Für die Frau. Milch, Käse, Wurstaufschnitt. Kleinkram. Was man wochentags eben so braucht zum Leben. Hat grad schon bezahlt und will losfahren. Da fällt ihm ein: ach ja, noch einen Sack Beuys für meine Anja. Das ist nicht seine Frau, das ist sein Hund. Geht also noch mal rein in den Laden, zu dem Fach mit der Tiernahrung. Beuys ist einfach am besten – und heute ausnahmsweise mit Rabatt. Leenders wirft den Sack in den Kofferraum, setzt sich hinters Steuer, startet und fährt hinunter zum Fluss. Die Wolken hängen tief, es wird Regen geben. Schon wieder. Er denkt an Anja und wie sie immer an ihm hochspringt. Er muss schmunzeln: Die merkt doch genau, was ich mitbringe.

Zurück ins Jahr 1974, New York, 409 West Broadway: Zusammen mit einem Kojoten verbringt Joseph Beuys drei Tage und drei Nächte in einem Ausstellungsraum der Galerie René Block. Im Verlauf der Aktion »I like America and America likes me« gewöhnen sich beide aneinander, tauschen schließlich ihr Lager: Der Kojote schläft auf der Filzdecke des Künstlers, Beuys legt sich aufs Stroh. Als er von »Little John« Abschied nimmt, ist aus dem Präriewolf fast so etwas wie ein Freund geworden.

Auch Rembrandt wäre eine Geschichte wert. Wenn man daran denkt, wie er mit hellen Lichtern das Rot einer Mütze, das Gold einer Brosche oder das Weiß eines Leinentuchs aus seinen dunklen Bildgründen holt. Würden uns seine Schönen – oder die seiner Zeitgenossen – befremden, lächelten sie uns, statt die Lippen geschlossen zu halten, mit blitzenden Zähnen zu? Und die Interieurs von Jan Vermeer. Mit der Spitzenklöpplerin, der Goldwägerin? Zarteste Bewegung ihrer Hände, Feinmotorik der täglichen Verrichtung. Konzentration allein aufs Gelingen des Werks. Oder hat vielleicht des

A little grocery store on the Lower Rhine. Somewhere between the German towns of Kalkar and Kleve. Flatland. Border country. A few simple shelves, a cooler, a magazine stand, and a lottery-ticket counter. It is shortly before closing. On the way home from work, Franz Leenders stops to get some groceries. Something he does every Wednesday, to help out his wife. Milk, cheese, cold cuts. A few things—whatever one needs to make it to the weekend. Franz has just paid and left the store when it occurs to him that he's forgotten to get a sack of Beuys for Anja. Anja is not his wife, but his dog. Franz goes back into the store and down the aisle to where the pet food is. Beuys is simply the best, and today it's even on sale. Franz again leaves the store, gets in his car, and drives down to the river. The clouds are hanging low in the sky. It's going to rain. Again. Franz thinks about Anja and how excited she gets when he comes home. "She always knows exactly what I've got in the bag," he thinks.

Back to the year 1974 and 409 West Broadway in Manhattan: together with a coyote, Joseph Beuys spends three days and three nights in an exhibition hall at the René Block Gallery. In the course of his performance "I like America and America likes me" the two get used to each other and even wind up exchanging their respective encampments: the coyote sleeps on the artist's felt blanket and Beuys on the coyote's straw. When it comes time depart the gallery, the two creatures, "Little John" the coyote and Beuys, have nearly become friends.

Rembrandt would also make for a good story—when one considers how he uses bright lights to conjure from his dark canvas the red of a cap, the gold of a brooch or the white of a sheet. Would his beauties—or those of his contemporaries—startle us if they were to smile back at us with sparkling white teeth instead of pursing their lips? And the interiors of Jan Vermeer. With the lacemaker and the goldweigher? The delicate movements of their hands as they perform their work with the utmost of precision. Or one could imagine

Malers Geograph beim Blick durchs Fenster grade eben dieses computergesteuerte Maschinenungetüm gleichen Namens und gleicher Präzision entdeckt? Und Yves Klein, der in seinen »Anthropometrien« auf am Boden liegenden Papierbahnen Körperabdrücke verewigte. Wie, wenn er statt seiner nackten weiblichen Modelle Fahrradreifen blau eingefärbt hätte? Und damit die Spuren anthropometrisch maßgefertigter Bikes in die Kunstgeschichte eingegangen wären?

Surreale Szenerien. Diametrale Welten. Auf der einen Seite ein Warenkorb mit Konsumgütern, Luxusartikeln, technischem Gerät. Auf der anderen Seite eine Künstlerliste vom Mittelalter bis zur Gegenwart, Namen, die für Werke stehen, legendär, umstritten, vergessen, aktuell. ArtBrands hat ein einfaches, aber denkbar strenges Prinzip: Berücksichtigt werden nur Produkte, die Namen von Künstlern tragen, und Künstler, von deren Namen es Produkte gibt. Fertig, mehr ist da nicht. Keine Überlegungen zum Wert, zur Qualität, Seltenheit oder persönlichen Vorliebe. Keine Kriterien, die zwischen Markt, Museen und privaten Sammlern die Kunst und deren permanenten Bedeutungswandel bestimmen. Nur ein Spiel, eine spielerische Versuchsanordnung aus Erfahrung und Erfindung. Mit spekulativen Verknüpfungen manchmal, bis hin zum ernsthaften Diskurs.

Über Beuys zum Beispiel: Löst sich die gesellschaftliche Sprengkraft seiner Botschaft, dem Menschen soziale und künstlerische Kompetenz zuzusprechen, ihm neue Energien zuzuführen, an Ursprünge zu erinnern, Zukunft zu ermöglichen, in ihrer ständigen Wiederholung auf? Hat sich ihr künstlerischer Anspruch in eine Marke verwandelt, die merkantilen Mechanismen unterliegt? Zähmt, domestiziert der Markt die Kunst? Vom Raubtier zum Haustier sozusagen? Sichtbar zuletzt als zufällige Metapher im namensgleichen Hundefutter? Doch lassen wir die Kirche im Dorf. Und Franz Leenders seinen verdienten Feierabend. Es ist ja nur ein Zufallskonstrukt, dieses Zusammentreffen des Ungleichen, von Kunst und Leben, von

the painter's Geographer casting a gaze out the window to discover a behemoth piece of computer-navigated equipment, also bearing the name of Vermeer? And Yves Klein whose "anthropometries" eternalized body impressions on paper and canvas? How would it have been if he had applied his dye to bicycle tires instead of naked female models so that the tracks made by anthropometrically tailor-made bikes might have gone into the history of art?

Surreal scenarios. Diametrically opposed worlds. On the one hand, a shopping cart with consumer goods, luxury articles, and technical equipment. On the other hand, a list of artists, extending from the Middle Ages to the present, names standing for legendary, controversial, forgotten, and current works. ArtBrands adheres to a strict, but straightforward principle: include products that share their names with artists and artists who share their names with products. That's it. No considerations of value, quality, rarity or personal preference. No criteria used to determine art and its continuously changing meaning in relation to markets, museums and private collectors. Only a game, a playful arrangement based on experience and discovery that sometimes offers speculative associations and points toward serious discourse.

In regard to Beuys, for instance. Does the societal explosiveness of his message, i.e. of attributing social and artistic competence to humans, supplying them with new forms of energy, reminding them of origins, enabling them a future, simply dissipate as a result of its continuous repetition? Has the artistic claim behind this message been transformed into a brand that is subject to market mechanisms? Does the marketplace ultimately tame and domesticate art? Transform it from a wild animal into a pet? Visible in the end as a chance metaphor in a brand of dog food of the same name? But let's not get carried away! And let us grant Franz Leenders a relaxing evening. It is only a chance construct, this convergence of unequals, of art and life, of

Dichtung und Wahrheit. Ein Märchen aus der Warenwelt. Wo kämen wir sonst hin?

Auf jeden Fall ins Museum. Dort schließlich landet ja alles, was Rang und Namen hat. Oder bekommen soll. Das sah auch Marcel Duchamp so, als er zu Beginn des vergangenen Jahrhunderts einen industriell gefertigten Flaschentrockner signierte, ihn, als »Readymade«, zum Kunstwerk erklärte. ArtBrands nun macht eine Weinflasche von Duchamp zur aktuellen Replik auf diesen kategorialen Kunstgriff von 1913, mit dem Unterschied allerdings, dass dieses Objekt – und mit ihm alle Objekte der Sammlung – gleichsam eine Zwillingssignatur trägt: die der jeweiligen Herstellerfirma und die von Michael Klant. Diese zweifache Autorschaft adelt das Werk in besonderem Maße. Es umgibt sich mit einer gedoppelten Aura, als wolle es mit derart verbriefter Qualität seiner prinzipiell unlimitierten Auflage spotten. Hier jedenfalls ist keine falsche Bescheidenheit angebracht. Der Name selbst, noch vor seiner ästhetischen Erscheinung, ist das Gütesiegel. Und einmal im musealen Kontext erlebt, einmal in künstlerischen Augenschein genommen, erreicht die Nobilitierung auch den Supermarkt. Und umgekehrt: Einmal im Warensortiment, in der Schaufensterauslage entdeckt, trifft die Banalisierung auch das Museum. Wahrnehmung im Wechselfieber. Kann man dann noch in der Londoner National Gallery das Doppelbildnis von Agostino und Niccolò de la Torre des florentinischen Renaissancekünstlers Lorenzo Lotto bewundern, ohne an ein Paar italienischer Fußballschuhe zu denken? Hat man dann nicht beim Brotkauf die Ackerfurchen von Anselm Kiefers Monumentalmalerei vor Augen? Oder fährt im Geiste mit »superscharfer« Messerklinge über die marmorglatten Oberflächen michelangelesker Skulptur? Grenzüberschreitungen ohne Ende. Und was bleibt noch von Picasso, wenn man täglich in seinem Namen zur Arbeit fährt?

Michael Klant hat sich dem Crossover verschrieben. Er ist Kunsthistoriker, Hochschullehrer, Verleger, Publizist, Sammler. Vor allem aber ist er Künstler: Fotograf, Filme- und Videomacher, Projekteplaner im öffentlichen Raum. Er lässt über Freiburg und Florida Flugzeuge mit Bannern kreisen, auf denen Ausschnitte des jeweils anderen Himmels zu sehen sind.

poetry and truth. A mere warehouse fairy tale. Where else would we wind up?

By all means in a museum. After all, that is where everybody who is anybody ultimately winds up. Or deserves to be regarded as such. That is the way Marcel Duchamp also saw things when he signed an industrially manufactured bottle dryer at the beginning of the past century and declared it, as a "readymade," a work of art. ArtBrands now turns a Duchamp wine bottle into a current replica that hearkens back to his categorical declaration from 1913, with the difference, however, being that this object—like all of the objects in the collection—bears a twin signature: that of the respective manufacturer and that of Michael Klant. This dual authorship ennobles the work. The work assumes a double aura, appearing to mock its essentially unlimited circulation from a position of attested quality. In any case, false modesty would not be appropriate here. The name itself, even before its aesthetic appearance, is the seal of approval. And once experienced in a museum setting, once examined from an artistic perspective, the ennoblement also extends to the supermarket. And vice versa: once discovered among common merchandise, in the store window, the banalization extends to the museum. A case of rapidly alternating perception. Will we still be able to admire the double portrait of Agostino and Niccolò de la Torre by the Florentine Renaissance artist Lorenzo Lotto in the London National Gallery without thinking about a pair of Italian soccer shoes? Will the image of the furrows in Anselm Kiefer's monumental painting accompany us when we go out to buy bread? Will we imagine a super-sharp razor passing over the smooth marble surface of a Michelangelo sculpture? Endless border crossings. And what remains of Picasso when we drive in a car bearing his name to work every day?

Michael Klant has dedicated himself to crossing borders. He is an art historian, college professor, publisher, journalist, and collector. He is primarily, however, an artist: a photographer, a film and video maker, a project planner at work in public spaces. He commissions pilots to tow banners showing a piece of the Florida sky over Freiburg and other pilots to tow banners showing a piece of the Freiburg sky over Florida. He photo-

Er fotografiert die Augen von Mitarbeitern einer Versicherung und hängt die Bilder mit irisierenden Farbkreisen um schwarze Pupillen als leuchtende Blicke vor deren Büros. Er entwirft Symbole für Weltmeisterschaftsstadien, um sie als ornamentale Schnittmuster in die Rasenflächen einmähen zu lassen. Er ist Regisseur eines Kinofilms, der die emanzipationspolitische Correctness, den »gegenderten« Mainstream im Hochschulalltag persifliert.

Michael Klant inszeniert Bilder, die unsere Wahrnehmung von Alltagserscheinungen subversiv lenken. In denen sich eingeschliffene Denk- und Sehweisen wie von selbst neu verbinden. Er arbeitet mit leichter Hand. Seine Handschrift sind formale Perfektion und Perspektivenwechsel. Er liebäugelt mit dem Laienblick. Und bietet vertrauten Motiven neue Auftrittsmöglichkeiten. Indem er ArtBrands, deren industriell gefertigte Produkte museal überhöht, setzt er nicht nur diese, sondern auch das Museumsinventar selbst unserer Aufmerksamkeit aus. Wie verhält es sich mit dem institutionellen Wertekanon des Sammelns, Bewahrens, Forschens und Vermittelns angesichts eines dem Massengeschmack angepassten Markts, seiner Schnäppchenstrategien und Genussversprechen? Was bedeuten Haltbarkeitsgarantien, wenn Verfallsdaten absatzsteigernd programmiert werden? Konservenkür und Konservatorenpflicht. Ewigkeitsanspruch. Wie positioniert sich Kunst im Wettbewerb mit kommerziellen Events und Kaufanreizen? Wie sehr besetzt Namedropping unsere Wahrnehmung? Immer erst der Blick auf das Schildchen. Die Bestätigung des schon Bekannten als Auswahlkriterium. Die Marke als Qualitätsmerkmal. Sicherheit geht vor!

ArtBrands befremdet. Verwandelt das Konsumvertraute in bildmäßige Erscheinungen, die sich unserer Nähe entziehen. Plötzlich fern aller Berührung ausgestellt, wird aus Distanz auch Differenz. Dieser feine Unterschied zwischen Wissen und Vermuten, diese innere Bewegung zwischen Haben und Begehren, die Räume öffnet zwischen uns und der wahren Welt. ∎

graphs the eyes of insurance company employees and hangs the pictures with iridescent rings around the black pupils as luminous gazes in front of their offices. He designs symbols for stadiums that have been selected as venues of the world soccer championships that are then mowed into the stadium grass as ornamental patterns. He is the director of a movie that satirizes the political correctness of the "gendered" mainstream of a college campus.

Michael Klant shows us images that subversively influence our perception of day-to-day phenomena. Images in which ingrained habits of thinking and seeing realign themselves as if of their own accord. He works with a light and deft hand. Formal perfection and alternating perspectives are his trademark. He tracks the layperson's view. And offers new venues for familiar motifs. By elevating ArtBrands, common industrially manufactured products, in the context of a museum exhibition, he exposes these and the regular museum inventory to our scrutiny. What is the state of the institutional values canon of collecting, conserving, researching and conveying in light of a market that is adapted to mass appeal, bargain-hunting strategies and promises of pleasure? What do shelf-life guarantees mean when best-by dates are programmed to promote turnover? A canned-goods cure and an obligation to conserve. A claim to eternity. How does art position itself in competition with commercial events and sales campaigns? To what extent is our perception influenced by name-dropping? Forever taking a look at the label first. The confirmation of what is already known as a selection criterion. The brand as a sign of quality. Safety comes first!

ArtBrands is disconcerting. It converts what is familiar to us as consumers into images that withdraw from us. Displayed beyond our reach, the sudden distance engenders a difference. This subtle distinction between knowledge and supposition, this inner movement between having and desiring that opens realms between us and the real world. ∎

Günter Figal

Im Namen der Kunst | In the Name of Art

Es gibt viele Dinge, die nach ihren Herstellern oder Erfindern benannt sind. Autos, Bleistifte und Regenmäntel sind nur einige von ihnen. Die Benennung ist nicht selten mit Hochschätzung verbunden. Dann muss über die Qualität des Produkts wenig gesagt werden – der Name spricht für sich. Oft wird freilich auch vergessen, dass es jemanden dieses Namens gab. Der Name ist dann nur mehr ein Etikett. Er dient zur Identifizierung der Sache.

Bei Kunstwerken ist es ähnlich und doch ganz anders. Auch hier steht der Name des Künstlers meist für das Werk. Ein Bild ist »ein Monet«, »ein Cézanne«, »ein Matisse«. Zwar scheint das Bild darin dem Auto ähnlich, das den Namen eines Ingenieurs oder Firmengründers trägt. Doch beim Bild die Verbindung ist enger, sie ist intensiver. Während das Auto auch dann

Many products are named after their inventors or manufacturers. Cars, pens, and raincoats are just a few. The name itself is often associated with a certain high regard. This makes it less important to focus on the quality of the product—the name speaks for itself. We often forget that there once was a person of the same name. The name has then become no more than a label that serves to identify a product.

In the case of works of art, it is both similar and altogether different. Here, too, the name of the artist often stands for the work of art. A painting is "a Monet," "a Cézanne," or "a Matisse." While the painting is similar in this regard to the car that bears the name of an engineer or a company founder, the connection between the artist and the painting is more intimate and intense. A car, for instance, may bear

Appel Cicero, 2000
Sardinen, 125 g
2,7 x 10,7 x 6,3 cm

Appel Cicero, 2000
Sardines, 125 g
2.7 x 10.7 x 6.3 cm

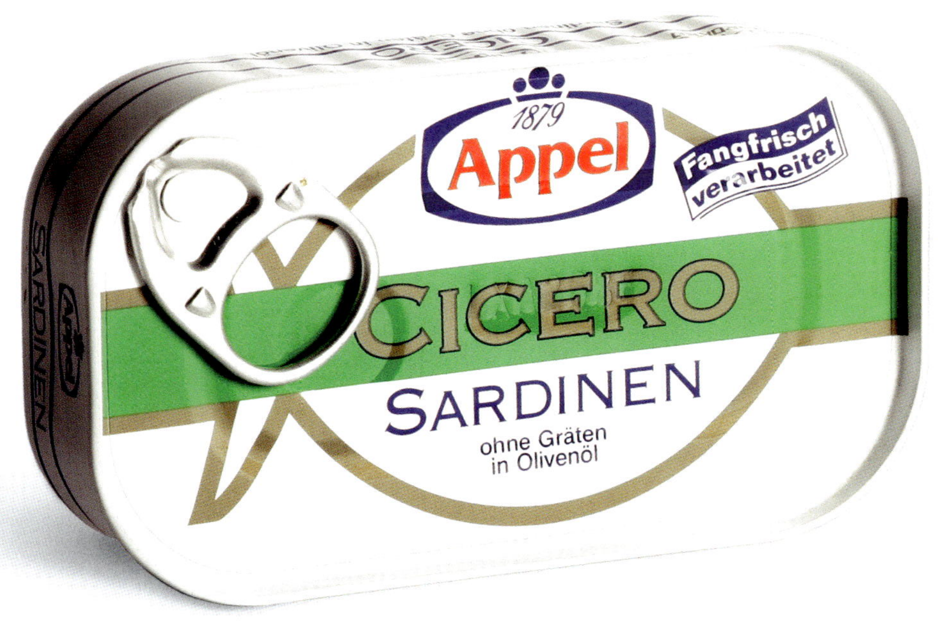
1879
Appel
Fangfrisch
verarbeitet
CICERO
SARDINEN
ohne Gräten
in Olivenöl
SARDINEN

noch seinen Namen behält, wenn das Produkt nichts mehr mit dem Träger des Namens zu tun hat, kann es keinen »Monet« geben, der nicht von Claude Monet gemalt wurde. Ein solches Bild wäre eine Fälschung. Der Künstlername eines Bildes ist niemals ein Etikett.

Bei Kunstwerken ist der Name kein Etikett, noch nicht einmal eine Qualitätsgarantie, sondern eine Bürgschaft; er steht für das Kunstwerk, indem er für dieses einsteht. Er verbürgt seine Echtheit. Die Farbe muss von der Hand des Künstlers aufgetragen worden sein, oder zumindest muss der Künstler, wie bei einer Druckgraphik, den Herstellungsvorgang überwacht und durch seine Signatur beglaubigt haben. Wenn sich erweist, dass ein Werk nicht von dem Künstler stammt, dem man es zuschrieb, ist das eine Minderung. Das Werk steht nun

the name of a company founder even though the company founder—long since passed away—had nothing to do with its production. This is not the case for works of art. There can be no "Monet" that was not painted by Claude Monet. Such a painting would be a forgery. The name of the artist who has created a work is never a mere label.

The name behind a work of art is not a label—and also not an assurance of quality—but a voucher. It stands for a work of art by assuming responsibility for it. It vouches for the work's authenticity. The paint must have been applied by the hand of the artist, or the artist will at least have had to monitor the production process—as in the case of a fine art print—and authenticate the work via signature. Works of art that turn out not stem from the artist they have been

Bayer Aspirin N2, 2007
20 Tabletten
Schachtel 1,7 x 8,9 x 4 cm

Bayer Aspirin N2, 2007
20 tablets
box 1.7 x 8.9 x 4 cm

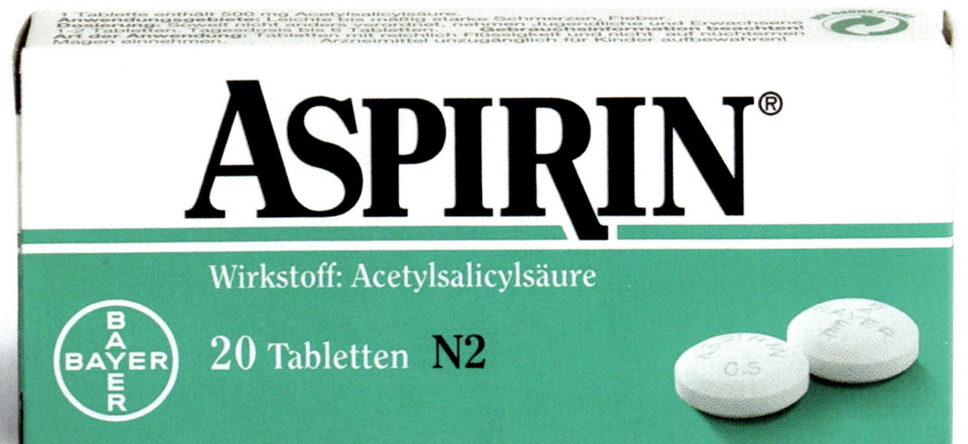

1 Tablette enthält 500 mg Acetylsalicylsäure.
Anwendungsgebiete: Leichte bis mäßig starke Schmerzen, Fieber.
Dosierung: Soweit nicht anders verordnet, nehmen Jugendliche und Erwachsene
1-2 Tabletten. Tagesdosis bis 6 Tabletten. Gebrauchsinformation beachten!
Art der Anwendung: Tabletten mit reichlich Flüssigkeit und nicht auf nüchternen
Magen einnehmen. Arzneimittel unzugänglich für Kinder aufbewahren!
ASPIRIN®
Wirkstoff: Acetylsalicylsäure
BAYER
20 Tabletten   N2

namenlos da – wie der einst so beliebte, inzwischen beinah vergessene »Mann mit dem Goldhelm«. Obwohl das Bild immer noch dasselbe ist, ist es nicht mehr dasselbe. Des Namens »Rembrandt« beraubt, ist es nicht mehr »echt«; es gilt nicht mehr als das Produkt einer besonderen und unverwechselbaren Hand. Man kann diese Hand nicht mehr mit einem Namen, der eine Bürgschaft ist, benennen.

Das heißt nicht, der Künstler sei wichtiger als seine Werke. Ohne die Werke wäre er eine mehr oder weniger normale bürgerliche Existenz, höchstens ein Künstlerdarsteller, also ein Anspruch ohne Einlösung. Ein wahrhafter Künstler bekundet sich in seinen Werken. Dabei stellt er seine Werke nicht einfach her, so dass sie als fertige eigentlich nichts mehr mit ihm zu tun haben. Der wahrhafte Künstler malt oder zeichnet

attributed to, and that are left nameless, are diminished—like the once so admired, but now almost forgotten painting "The Man with the Gold Helmet." Although the painting is still the same, it is no longer the same. Bereft of the name "Rembrandt," it is no longer "authentic." It no longer qualifies as the work of a special and unique hand. One can no longer name this hand with a name that is a voucher.

This doesn't mean that artists are more important than their works. Without works, artist aspirants might at most play the role of an artist, thereby issuing a claim that cannot be redeemed. True artists express themselves in their works. In doing so, they do not simply produce works that no longer have anything to do with them as individuals once they are complete. True artists paint or draw themselves entirely into

Dr. Beckmann Anti-Grau, 2005
Waschmittel
13,3 x 11,2 x 3,1 cm

Dr. Beckmann Anti-Gray, 2005
Detergent
13.3 x 11.2 x 3.1 cm

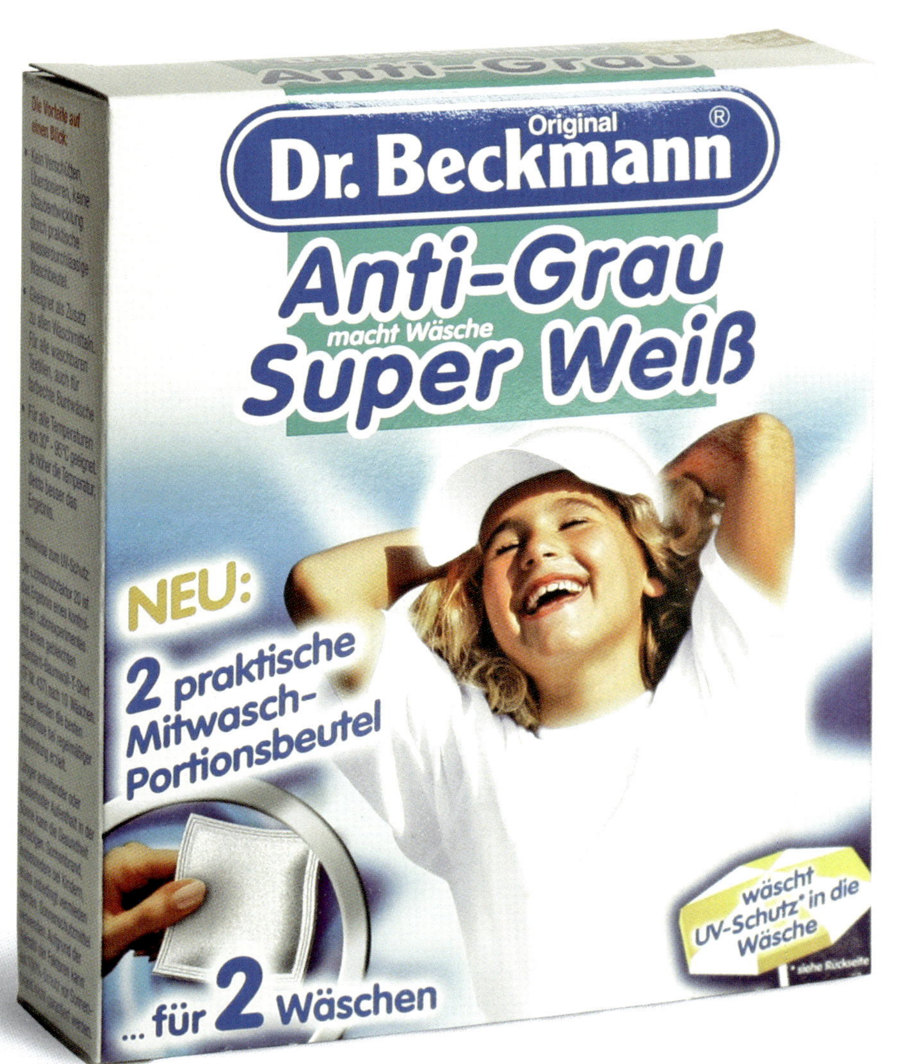

Anti-Grau
Original
Dr. Beckmann ®
Anti-Grau
macht Wäsche
Super Weiß
NEU:
2 praktische
Mitwasch-
Portionsbeutel
... für 2 Wäschen
wäscht
UV-Schutz* in die
Wäsche
* siehe Rückseite

sich vollkommen in seine Werke ein. So wird die Person des Künstlers dinghaft, sie vergegenständlicht sich; der Künstler überträgt sein leibhaftes Dasein, sein Auge und die Bewegung seiner Hand, in das Kunstwerk, das nun für ihn, für seine Leibhaftigkeit, steht; allein das Werk seiner Hand kann die Einmaligkeit seines leibhaften Daseins erweisen und bewahren. Alles, was im Leben eines Künstlers nichts mit seinem Werk zu tun hat, ist letztlich belanglos, Anekdote. Der Künstler wird und ist Werk. Statt dass eine Skulptur, wie die Pygmalions, lebendig wird, wird der Künstler zu Farbe oder Stein. So ist es nur konsequent, dass er auch seinen Namen dem Werk gibt – dass er ihn an das Werk übergibt.

Daher kommt die Verblüffung, das amüsierte Erstaunen, wenn der Name an Dingen vorkommt, die keine Werke des

their works. They transfer or infuse their incarnate existence, their gaze and the movement of their hands, into the work of art that then stands for them, for their incarnate selves. The work of their hands alone can give testimony to and conserve the uniqueness of their incarnate existence. Everything in the lives of artists that has nothing to do with their works is ultimately of no immediate regard, an anecdote. Artists emerge and exist in their works. Instead of sculptures transforming into living beings like Pygmalion's Galatea, it is artists who become paint or stone. It is therefore only appropriate that artists give their names to their works—that they transfer their names to their works.

This is the source of our astonishment and amusement when we see the name of artists on things that were not created

Bellini, Il Cocktail di Venezia, 2000
0,75 l-Flasche
Höhe 32,5 cm, ⌀ 8,5 cm

Bellini, The Venetian Cocktail, 2000
0.75 l bottle
height: 32.5 cm, ⌀ 8.5 cm

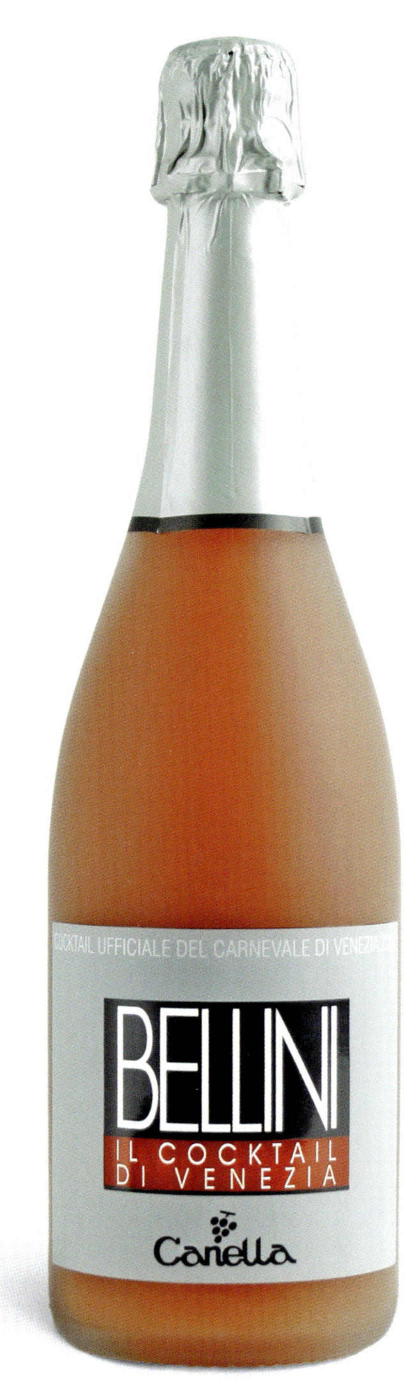

Künstlers und noch nicht einmal Kunstwerke sind. Dabei sind Verblüffung und Erstaunen umso größer, je tiefer der Name des Künstlers in sein Werk eingegangen und dabei zum Namen des Werkes geworden ist. Dass auch andere Personen wie der Künstler heißen, ist nicht erstaunlich; dass er Familie, Nachkommen, Namensvettern hat, nimmt man als selbstverständlich zur Kenntnis; es gehört auf die andere Seite der Künstlerperson, zu deren bürgerlicher Existenz. Doch eine Forstmaschine, die »Vermeer« heißt, ist erstaunlich, ebenso wie der Sack Hundefutter mit dem Namen »Beuys«. Die für sich genommen harmlosen Alltagsdinge werden durch ihre Namen zu Travestien der Kunst.

Das geschieht nicht durch den Namen allein, sondern erst durch die Verbindung von Name und Ding. Durch diese Verbin-

by them and are not even works of art. This astonishment is yet more profound the deeper the names of the artists have gone into their works and have come to stand for the works. The fact that other persons share the name of the artist is not astonishing. We simply acknowledge that artists have immediate families, relatives, children, and other namesakes. Such facts belong to the other side of artists' lives, to their normal existence as persons. On the other hand, a piece of logging equipment that bears the name "Vermeer" or a sack of dog food that bears the name "Beuys" is astonishing. Such prosaic items, harmless in and of themselves, are turned into travesties of art in virtue of their names.

This happens the moment we draw the association between the name and the product. For a brief moment, the product

Beuys Dog Mix, 2005
Hundefutter, 20 kg
80 x 54 x 25 cm

Beuys Dog Mix, 2005
Dog food, 20 kg
80 x 54 x 25 cm

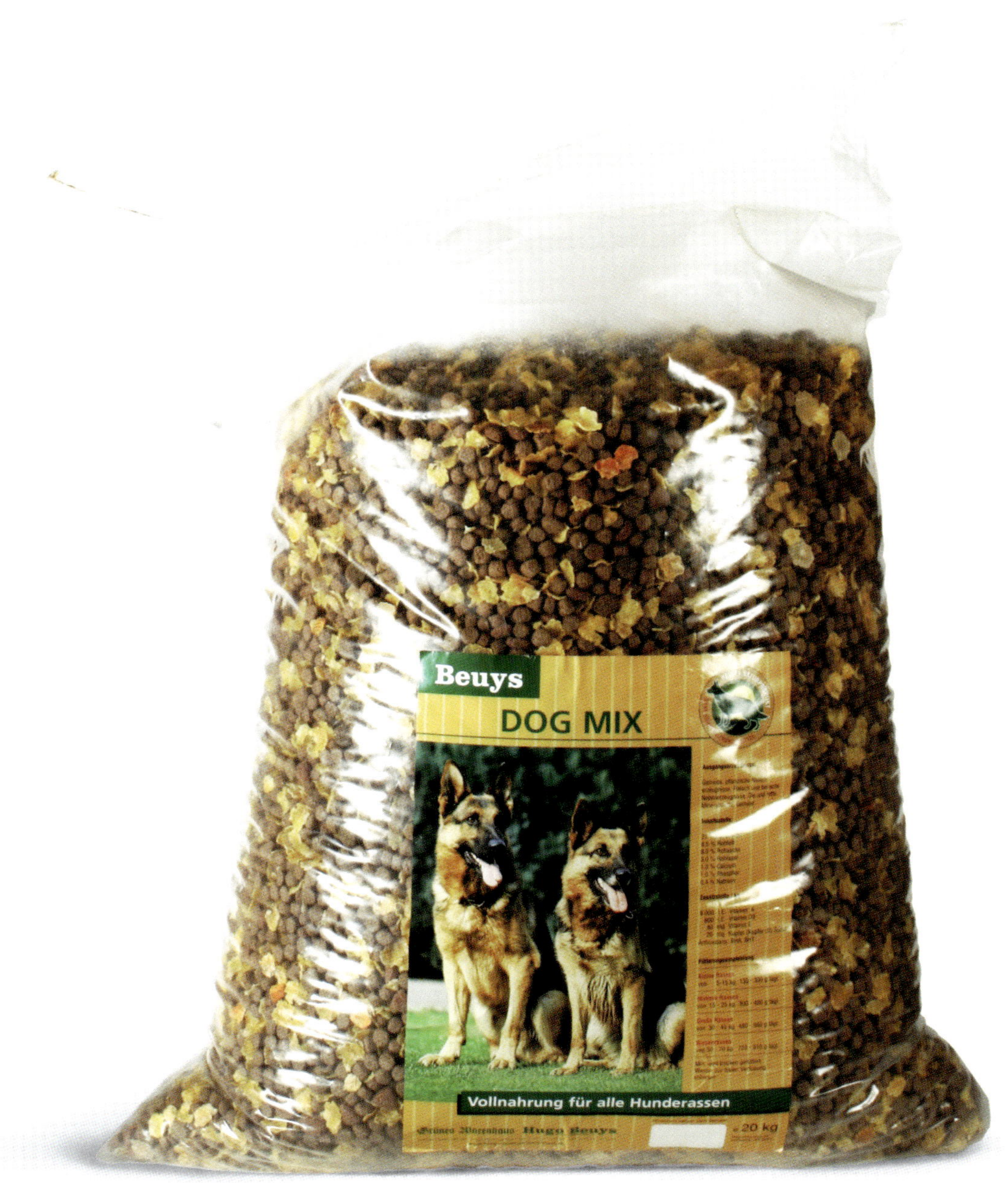
Beuys
DOG MIX
Vollnahrung für alle Hunderassen
Hugo Beuys
20 kg

dung geben die Dinge sich für einen kurzen Moment wie ein
Kunstwerk, um zugleich, wie mit verlegenem Lachen, einzuge-
stehen, dass sie keine Kunstwerke sind. Einen Augenblick lang
mag die Verbindung aufleuchten und einleuchtend sein. In der
Tat kann die erdige Farbe und Konsistenz des Hundefutters an
Filz und Fett erinnern, und man wird die Vorstellung, dass der
Erfinder oder Finder des Fettstuhls auch dieser Substanz plasti-
sche Qualität abgewonnen hätte, nicht ganz abwegig finden.
Dennoch: Das Ding, das ein banales Gebrauchsding ist und
einen Künstlernamen trägt, stellt den Namen nur aus. Es zerrt
ihn gleichsam hervor und gibt ihn der Heiterkeit preis. Es ist,
als ob jemand in einer Robe aufträte, die ihm nicht zusteht – in
einem echten Amtskleid beim Karneval.

appears to the beholder to be a work of art, only to withdraw
back into its ordinariness the very next moment with a laugh.
The association may linger for a moment, appearing to be
plausible. Indeed, the earthy color and consistency of the dog
food may remind the beholder of felt and fat, or some other
substance the creator of "Fat Chair" might have used. However, the thing that is a common product and that bears the
name of an artist merely exhibits the name. It pushes the name
to the front and center and makes it a subject of amusement.
It is like the person who appears at the Mardi Gras parade in
an official robe he is not otherwise entitled to wear.

The name of the artist will have to have thoroughly suffused
the accompanying work in order to withstand such exposure.

Breuer Comforta, 2007
Runddusche
190 x 100 x 100 cm

Breuer Comforta, 2007
Round shower
190 x 100 x 100 cm

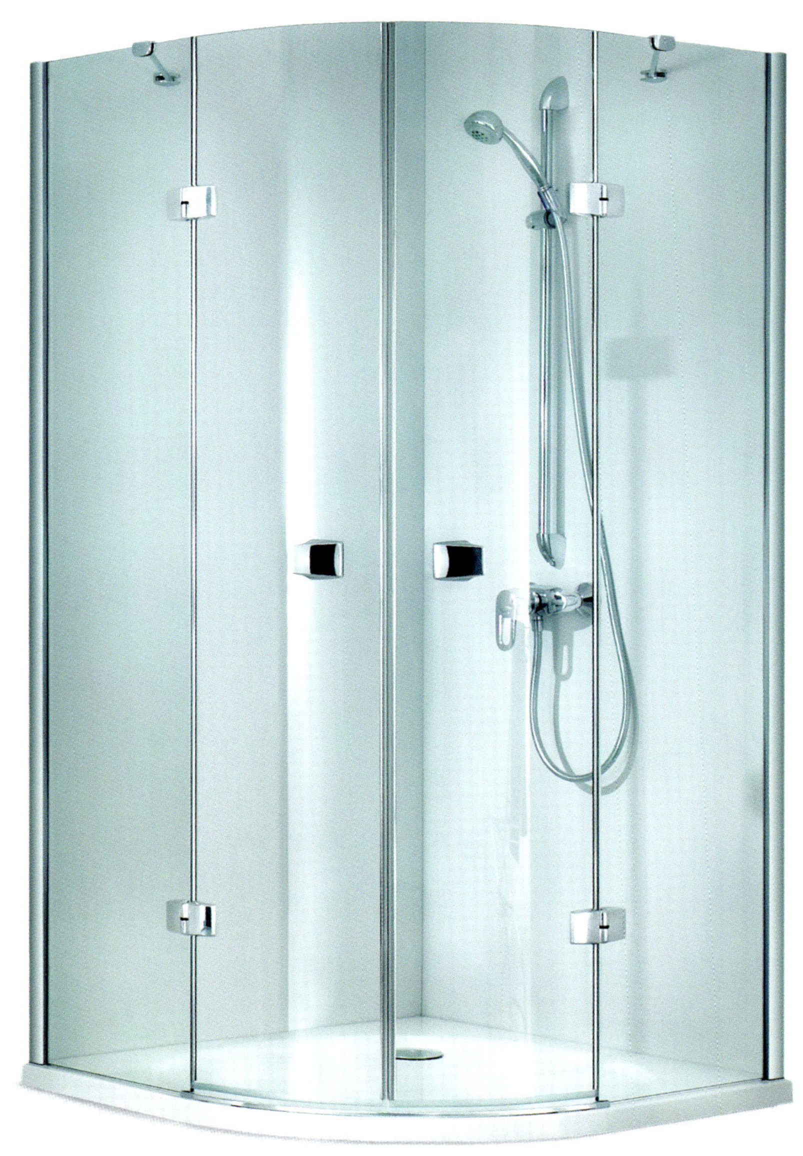

Der Künstlername muss tief in die ihm zugehörigen Dinge eingesenkt sein, damit er das aushält. Dann freilich weist er das Ding, dem oder dessen Verpackung er in aller Unschuld aufgedruckt wurde, in seine Schranken. Der Name gibt unmissverständlich zu verstehen, dass dieses Ding nur ein Trommelhäcksler, dass es nur ein Sack Hundefutter ist. Es ist, als werde dem Ding die Robe, die es wie ein übermütig oder dreist gewordener Narr zur Schau trug, wieder abgenommen. Es reicht, nun ist es genug.

Also muss ein Ding seinen Namen wert sein. Es muss das Ergebnis einer Verwandlung sein – der Vergegenständlichung leibhaften Daseins, damit ein Name für es mehr als ein Etikett ist. Schon ein solides Handwerksprodukt hat etwas davon; es lobt seinen Meister. Doch allein Kunstwerke sind Dinge,

Then, of course, it duly puts the common product that bears its name in its place. The name signals unmistakably that this object is only a brush chipper or a sack of dog food. The object is then like the intoxicated court jester who is suddenly divested of the official robe he has been brazenly parading around in. Enough is enough!

We can conclude that an object must be worthy of its name. It must be the result of a process of transformation—the hypostatization of incarnate existence—in order to ensure that the name for it is more than a label. While the work of a careful craftsman may come close—it will praise its master—only works of art are instantiations of incarnate life, products of the metamorphosis of eye and hand to paint and stone. The astonishing nature of this metamorphosis is illuminated in the

Canaletto / Caravaggio / Donatello, 2006
Steuergeräte für die Physiotherapie aus der Serie Grandi maestri
Iontophoresis / Interferenz-Elektrotherapie / Ultraschall-Therapie
je 38 x 25 x 23 cm

Canaletto / Caravaggio / Donatello, 2006
Physical therapy control units from the Grandi Maestri series
Iontophoresis / Interferential Therapy / Ultrasound Therapy
each unit: 38 x 25 x 23 cm

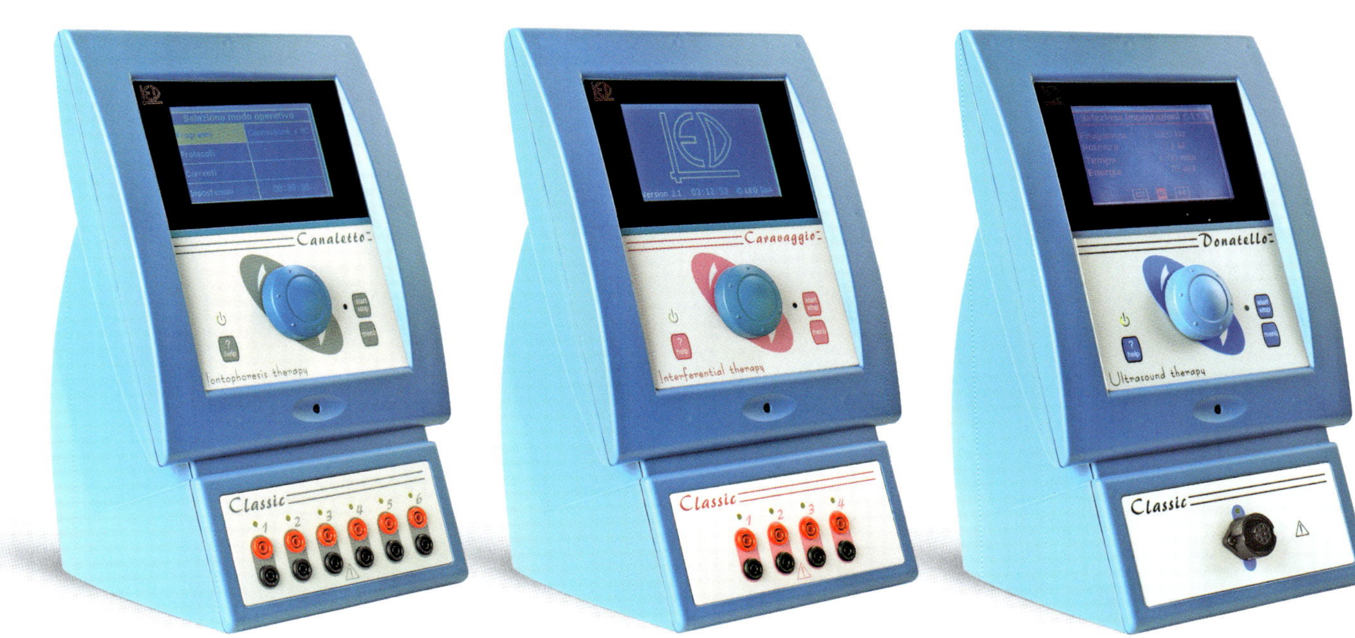
Canaletto
Iontophoresis therapy
Classic
Caravaggio
Interferential therapy
Classic
Donatello
Ultrasound therapy
Classic

die zum Gegenstand gewordenes Leben sind, Metamorphosen von Auge und Hand zu Farbe und Stein. Im planvollen
Vorzeigen der Travestie, wie es in den Arbeiten von Michael
Klant geschieht, in der ironischen Geste, die banale Dinge mit
unpassendem großen Namen vorweist, scheint die Erstaun-
lichkeit dieser Metamorphosen auf. Das gibt diesem Vorzeigen
die Tiefe der Kunst. Im Durchschauen der Travestie ist das
Geheimnis der Kunst zu ahnen: ihre das Leben in die Dinge
versetzende Magie. ■

planned display of travesty we see in the works of Michael
Klant, in the ironic gesture that associates banal things with
great names. This gives the present exhibition the depth of
art. In comprehending this travesty, a premonition of the mys-
tery of art is won: the infusing of material with life. ■

Cellini Espressotasse, 2004
Tasse, Höhe 4,3 cm, ⌀ 5,3 cm
Untertasse, Höhe 1,3 cm, ⌀ 12 cm

Cellini Espresso Cup, 2004
Cup, height: 4.3 cm, ⌀ 5.3 cm
Saucer, height: 1.3 cm, ⌀ 12 cm

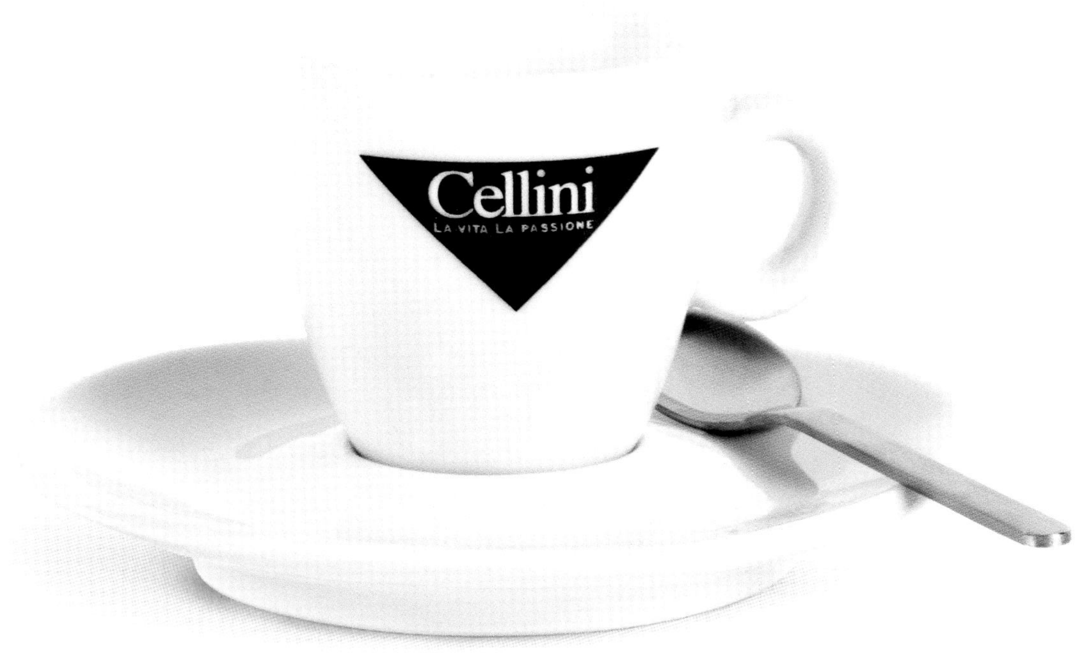
Cellini
LA VITA LA PASSIONE

Michael Klant

Consumo, ergo sum artista | Consumo, Ergo Sum Artista

New York, Oktober 1997. Beim Kofferauspacken merke ich, dass ich die Zahnpasta zuhause vergessen habe. Zum Glück ist der Drugstore noch geöffnet: Colgate, Pepsodent, Mentadent, Sensodyne, Rembrandt. Rembrandt? »Whitening toothpaste« steht auch noch auf der Schachtel – dabei weiß doch jeder, dass Rembrandt in Brauntönen gemalt hat. Ich greife zu Colgate.

Am nächsten Tag gehe ich in den Drugstore zurück, Rembrandt kaufen. Bis heute habe ich die Tube nicht angebrochen. Das kann ich nicht von allen Objekten mit Künstlernamen

New York, October 1997. While unpacking my suitcase I notice that I must have forgotten my toothpaste at home. It's a good thing the drugstore is still open: Colgate, Pepsodent, Mentadent, Sensodyne, Rembrandt. Rembrandt? No kidding, the box says "Whitening Toothpaste." But everyone knows that Rembrandt painted in tones of brown. I reach for Colgate.

On the next day, I went back to the drugstore to buy Rembrandt—a tube of toothpaste that I have left unopened to this very day. I can't say the same about all of the other pro-

David Sonnenblumenkerne, 1998
106-g-Tüte
18,9 x 10,2 x 2,5 cm

David Sunflower Seeds, 1998
106 g bag
18.9 x 10.2 x 2.5 cm

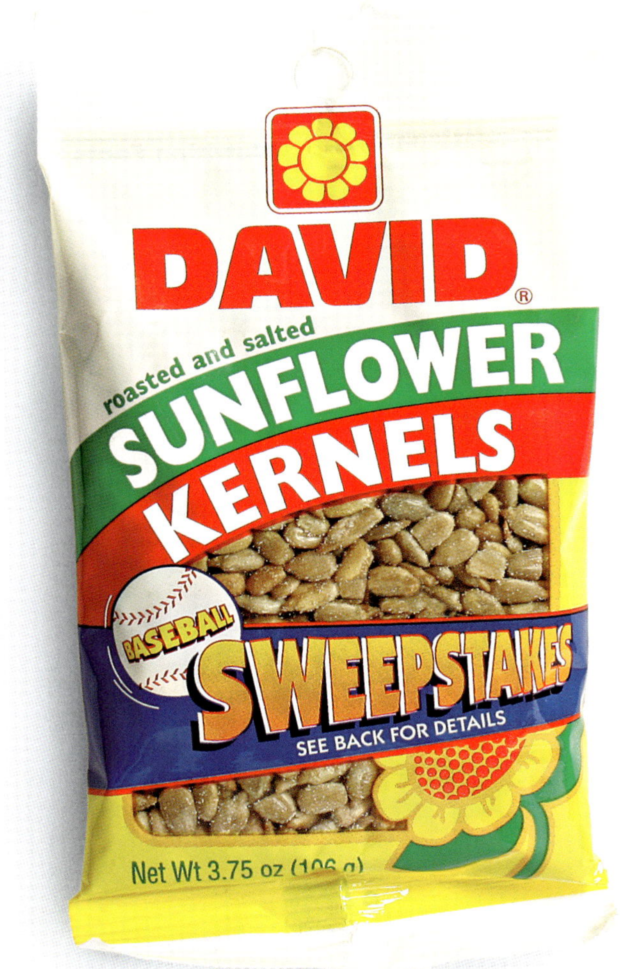

DAVID
roasted and salted
SUNFLOWER
KERNELS
BASEBALL
SWEEPSTAKES
SEE BACK FOR DETAILS
Net Wt 3.75 oz (106 g)

sagen, die ich seither erstanden habe. Die Wiener Würstchen von Goya aus Florida sind mir ausgezeichnet bekommen. In der Schweiz verzehre ich gern die zuckerfreien Stella-Kekse. Auch der Grappa Caravaggio, erhältlich in jedem deutschen Penny Markt, ist eine Empfehlung wert. Der Besuch der Biennale in Venedig lässt sich gut mit dem Genuss eines Bellini-Cocktails verbinden. Ich kann von mir behaupten, dass ich wichtige Künstlernamen nicht nur aus dem Lexikon oder aus dem Museum kenne, sondern genauso vom Geschmack.

Große Namen billig zu erwerben, bringt doppelten Genuss: Zum Finderglück kommt die Genugtuung, dem Kunstmarkt ein Schnäppchen geschlagen zu haben. Ein Giotto-Klebestift ist mir so wertvoll wie eines seiner Gemälde. Die kleine Espressotasse von Cellini bringt mir die Perseus-Statue von der

ducts bearing the names of artists that I've acquired since. The Vienna sausage by Goya that I bought in Florida was really very tasty. When I'm in Switzerland, I like to eat the sugar-free Stella cookies. Caravaggio grappa, available in any Penny Market in Germany, is altogether drinkable. And a visit to the Biennale in Venice can be very well combined with the enjoyment of a Bellini cocktail. I can attest that I have become familiar with the names of many important artists not from textbooks and museums alone, but also from an array of tastes.

Acquiring big names cheaply is a double pleasure: in addition to the joy of making a discovery, there is the satisfaction of having played a trick on the art market. A Giotto glue stick is as valuable to me as one of his paintings. The little espresso cup by Cellini has a way of transporting the statue of Perseus

Dove Extra Sensitive, 1998
Feuchtigkeitscreme, 0,2 l
12,5 x 9,2 x 3,9 cm

Dove Extra Sensitive, 1998
Moisturizing Cream, 0.2 l
12.5 x 9.2 x 3.9 cm

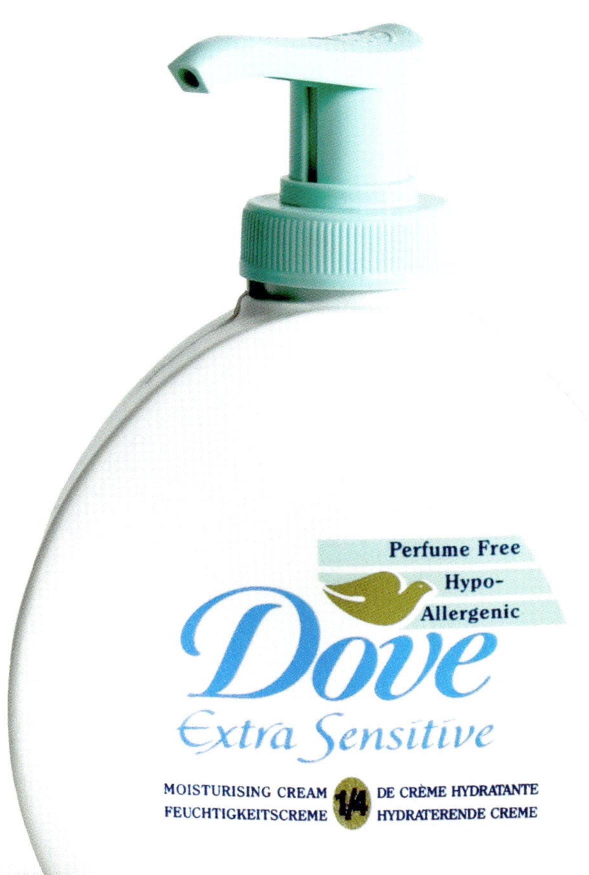
Perfume Free
Hypo-
Allergenic
Dove
Extra Sensitive
MOISTURISING CREAM
FEUCHTIGKEITSCREME
1/4
DE CRÈME HYDRATANTE
HYDRATERENDE CREME

Piazza della Signoria in Florenz nach Hause. Wenn ich Olivenöl von Viola erwerbe, kaufe ich Videokunst mit ein. So laden sich die Produkte magisch auf und rufen ein ganzes »musée imaginaire« (André Malraux) hervor. Wer sagt denn, dass nicht auch massenweise produzierte Dinge eine Aura haben können? Das eine Stück, das ich besitze: mein Unikat.

Ich ertappe mich dabei, wie ich lieber in Supermärkte gehe als in Kunstausstellungen. Meine Frau musste beim Einkaufen schon viel Geduld mit mir aufbringen. Mittlerweile habe ich auch Freunde angesteckt. Statt mir von Museumsbesuchen im Ausland zu berichten, überreichen sie mir ArtBrands als Mitbringsel. Auf Reisen hat man schnell heraus, welche Kaufhausabteilungen die wichtigsten sind. Während z. B. Haushaltsartikel von wenigen Global Players monopolistisch besetzt

from the Piazza della Signoria in Florence to my kitchen at home. When I buy a bottle of Viola olive oil, I simultaneously acquire a work of video art. As if magically charged, the products evoke an entire "musée imaginaire" (André Malraux). Who says that things that are mass produced can't have an aura? The one item that I possess is my unique specimen.

Sometimes I catch myself being a lot happier about going to supermarkets than art exhibitions. My wife has to show a lot of patience whenever we go shopping together. I've noticed that friends of mine have also gotten the bug. Instead of reporting to me about their visits to museums abroad, they bring me ArtBrands as souvenirs. When traveling, one quickly learns what store departments are the most important. While departments for household products seem to have been mo-

Dreher

Drei Bierflaschen à 0,33 l

20,5 x 18 x 6 cm

Dreher

Three 0.33-liter bottles of beer

20.5 x 18 x 6 cm

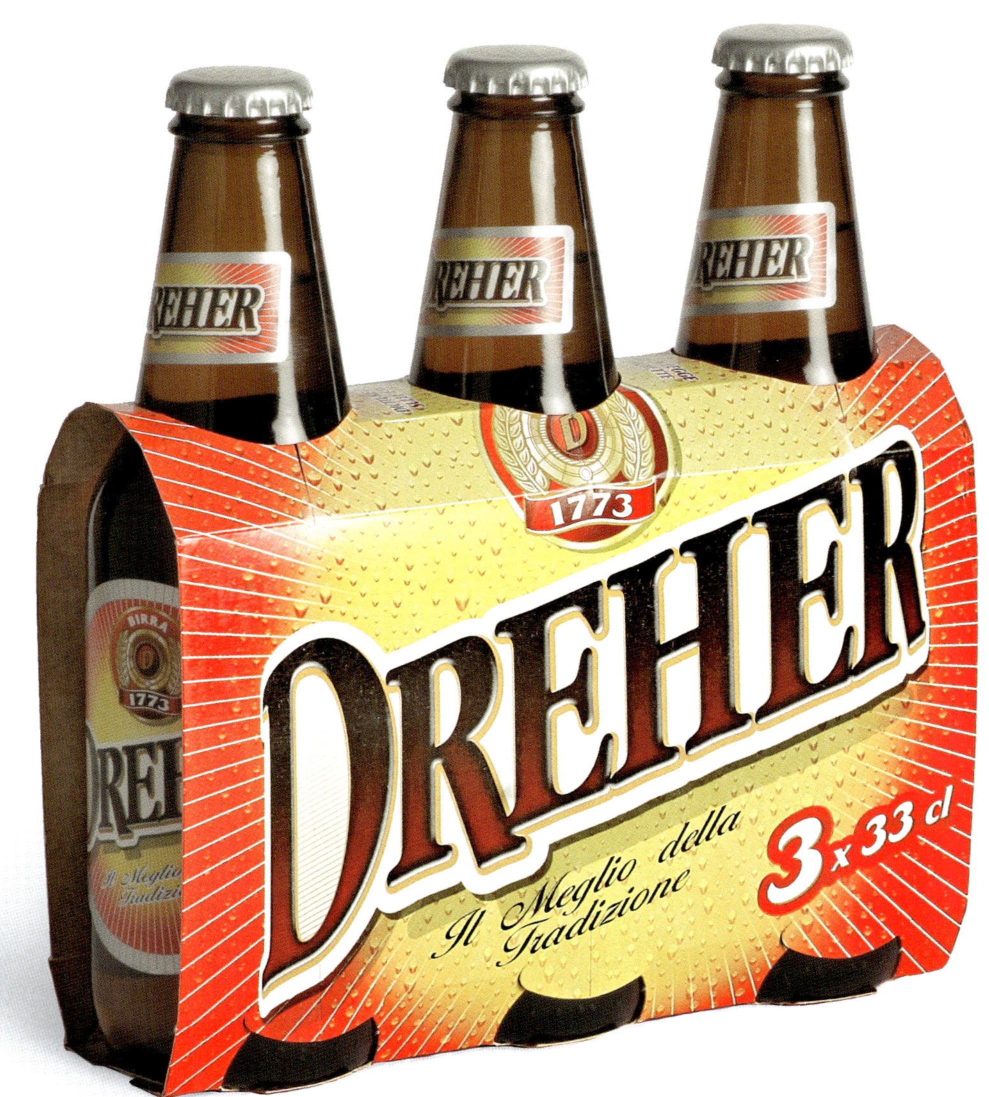
DREHER
DREHER
DREHER
BIRRA
1773
DREHER
Il Meglio della Tradizione
1773
DREHER
Il Meglio della Tradizione
3 x 33 cl

sind, trifft man bei Speisen und Getränken auf immer neue Namen von regionalen Anbietern. Ja, ArtBrands tauchen hier so zahlreich auf, dass man ganze Speisekarten damit füllen kann.

Manches liegt indessen greifbar nah und bedarf nur der Beachtung. So fragt mich Künstlerfreund Timm Ulrichs anlässlich eines Besuchs, ob er die Augen mit offen halten soll – und kommt am nächsten Morgen mit der Dove-Lotion aus dem Gästezimmer. Natürlich: Arthur Dove, Begründer der abstrakten Malerei in Amerika. Darauf hätte ich selber kommen müssen. Ob er bekannt genug ist, um in die Sammlung aufgenommen zu werden? Und: ob sich die Kunstgeschichte über Künstlernamen darstellen lässt? Immerhin beruht die frühe Kunstgeschichtsschreibung, das Buch »Le vite« von Giorgio Vasari, auf Künstlerbiografien.

nopolized by a small number of global players, food & beverage shelves abound with the ever changing names of regional suppliers. ArtBrands are so numerous here that you could fill entire menus with them.

Some things mysteriously escape one's attention. Timm Ulrichs, an artist friend of mine, asked me once while spending the weekend whether I'd appreciate it if he, too, kept an eye out—and then appeared for breakfast the next morning holding a dispenser of Dove lotion from our guest bathroom. "Of course, Arthur Dove, one of the founders of abstract painting in America!" I should have gotten that one. Is Dove famous enough to make it into the collection? Can the history of art be represented using the names of artists? After all, as is evidenced by Giorgio Vasari's book "Le vite," early art history is based on the biographies of artists.

Duchamp, 2002

Syrah Wein, 1,5 l Magnum-Flasche

Höhe 35,5 cm, ø 10,8 cm

Duchamp, 2002

Syrah wine, magnum bottle

height: 35.5 cm, ø 10.8 cm

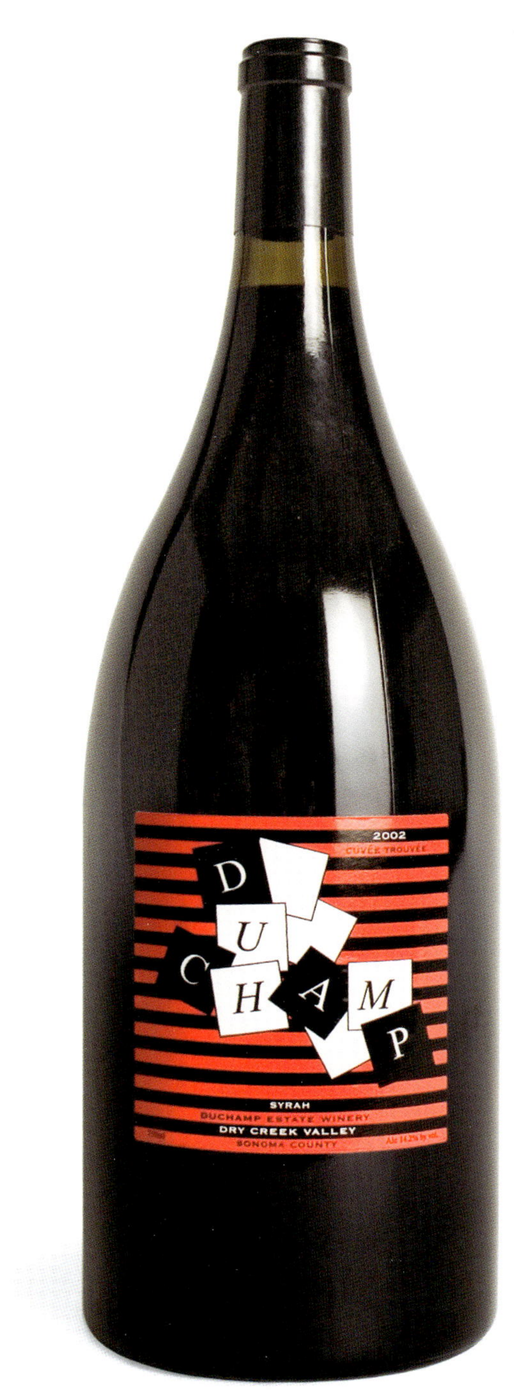
2002
CUVÉE TROUVÉE
DUCHAMP
SYRAH
DUCHAMP ESTATE WINERY
DRY CREEK VALLEY
SONOMA COUNTY
Alc 14.2% by vol.

Nach einem selbst aufgestellten Künstleralphabet beginne ich zu recherchieren. Im Internet stoße ich auf Lichtenstein und erwerbe in der Apotheke daraufhin mein kleinstes Objekt, ein Vitamin B12-Präparat. Die Walther-Pistole habe ich bei ebay ersteigert. Auch vom Manet-Motorroller, einem slowakischen Produkt der späten 1950er-Jahre, habe ich durch eine Website Kenntnis bekommen. Ich stelle mir den Künstler, der gern mit Gehrock und Zylinder durch Paris flanierte, auf dem wendigen Stadt-Scooter vor. Er wird überholt von Monet, dem Bohémien, auf einer schweren 500er Monet-Goyon, die den Pleinair-Maler mit sattem Brummen hinaus nach Argenteuil befördert.

Es bilden sich zwei Kategorien heraus: Dort, wo der Hersteller der Ware selbst einen Künstlernamen trägt, handelt es sich um Originale. Nachträglich und absichtsvoll mit Künstlerna-

After devising a glossary of artists from A-Z, I begin to research. On the Internet I happen upon Lichtenstein and then go out and acquire my smallest object, a vial of Lichtenstein vitamin B12 solution, at a local pharmacy. The Walther pistol, I acquire via eBay. I also learn of the Manet scooter, a Slovakian product from the late 1950s, on the Internet. I imagine the artist, who was fond of strolling through Paris in a frock coat and top hat, zipping about the city on the scooter, only to be passed by Monet, the bohémien, on a powerful and throaty 500cc Monet Goyon that transports the pleinair painter out to Argenteuil.

Two distinct categories emerge: products whose manufacturers happen to share the name of a famous artist (originals) and products that have been given the name of a famous

Ernst, 2007
Katalysator
9,5 x 104,1 x 20,5 cm

Ernst, 2007
Catalytic converter
9.5 x 104.1 x 20.5 cm

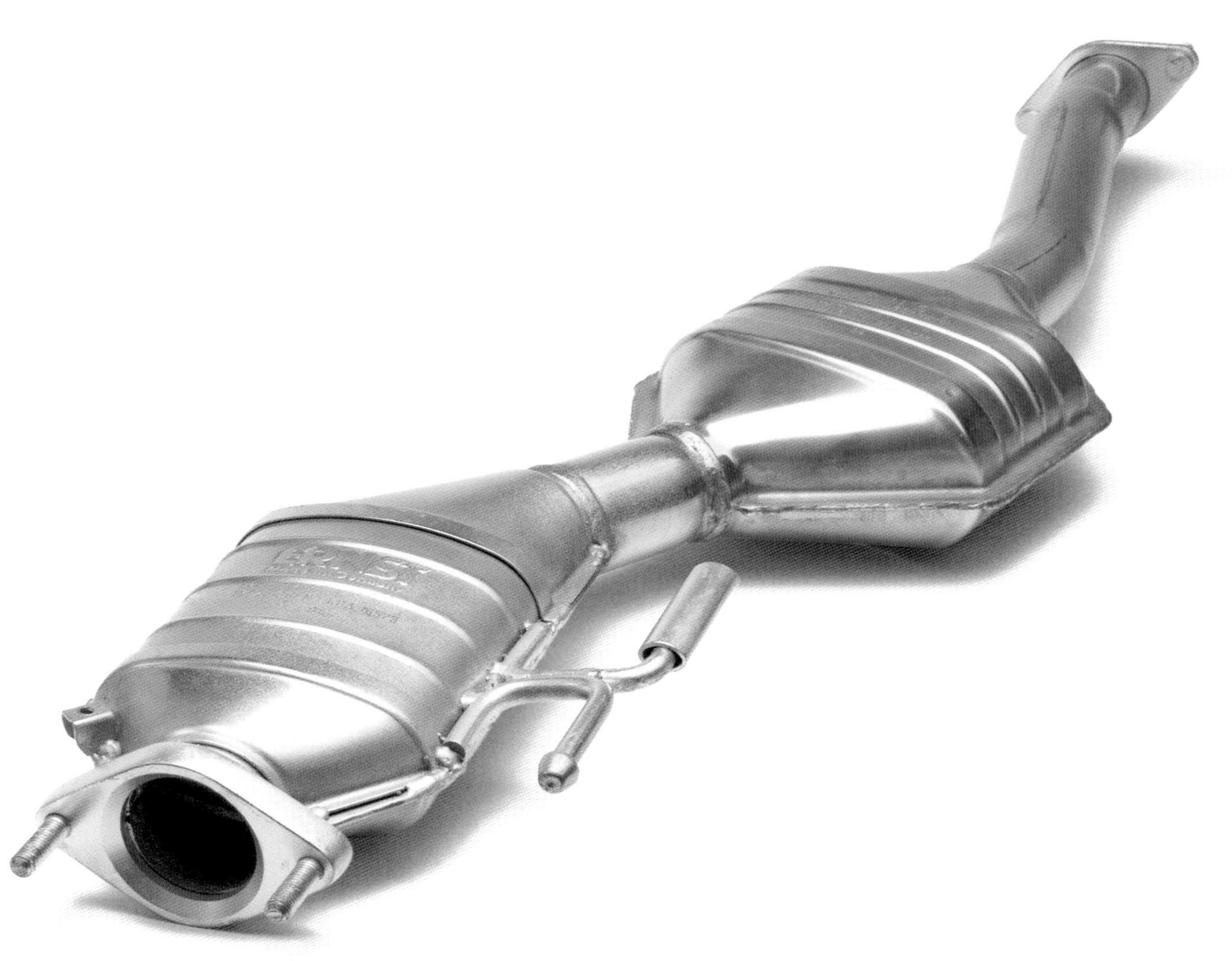

men bezeichnete Produkte sind dagegen Fälschungen, sofern sie nicht autorisiert sind. Allerdings scheinen gerade die Erstgenannten der Kunst abtrünnig geworden zu sein. Dieses berufliche Fremdgehen ist, kunstgeschichtlich betrachtet, wiederum nichts Neues. Der Kunstsoziologe Arnold Hauser berichtet, dass es im Holland des 17. Jahrhunderts – einer frühen bürgerlichen Gesellschaft, in der Künstler bereits den Gesetzen des freien Marktes unterworfen waren – zu einem Kunstproletariat kam, was die meisten Maler zwang, »neben ihrem künstlerischen Beruf auch zu einem anderen Verdienst zu greifen.« Jan Steen und Vermeer waren Schenkwirte, Hobbema betätigte sich als Steuereintreiber, van Goyen handelte mit Tulpen. Rembrandt starb verarmt.

artist (forgeries). Interestingly enough, it is the originals that seem to have broken more definitively with the world of art. From a historical perspective, this professional infidelity is nothing new. The art sociologist Arnold Hauser has suggested that an art proletariat developed in 17th century Holland—an early bourgeois society in which artists were subject to the laws of a free-market economy—which forced most painters "to seek other forms of gainful employment." Jan Steen and Vermeer were tavern operators, Hobbema was a tax collector, and van Goyen was a tulip trader. Rembrandt died in poverty.

Are the manufacturers of Rembrandt toothpaste and Vermeer agricultural machines perhaps relatives of the artists? This has been confirmed in the case of Beuys dog food, which was de-

Fini's Feinstes, 2007
Weizenmehl, 1000 g
15,5 x 12 x 7,3 cm

Fini's Finest, 2007
Wheat flour, 1000 g
15.5 x 12 x 7.3 cm

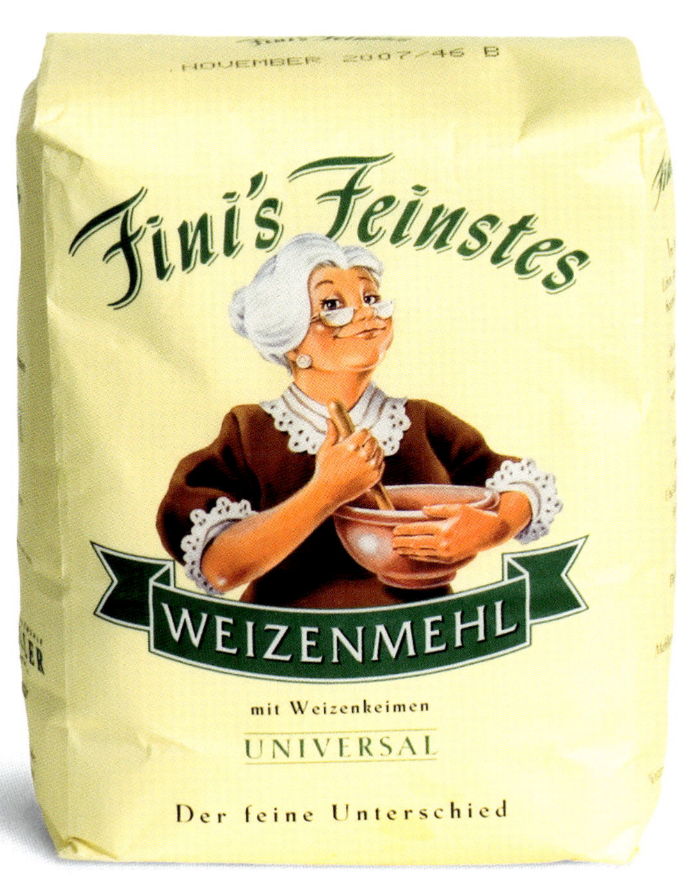
NOVEMBER 2007/46 B
Fini's Feinstes
WEIZENMEHL
mit Weizenkeimen
UNIVERSAL
Der feine Unterschied

Liegen bei der Rembrandt-Zahnpasta oder den Landmaschinen von Vermeer womöglich verwandtschaftliche Verhältnisse zu den Künstlern vor? Verbürgt ist dies für das Beuys-Hundefutter, das ein Cousin von Joseph Beuys entwickelt hat. Die Konzeptkünstlerin Hanne Darboven entstammt der traditionsreichen Hamburger Kaffee-Dynastie. Die Plastikerin Vera Röhm kommt aus dem Hause Röhm Plexiglas. Picasso-Parfüm gibt es von seiner Tochter Paloma. Niki de St. Phalle kreierte eine eigene Linie.

Vor der Qual der Wahl steht man bei unterschiedlichen Dingen mit demselben Herstellernamen, etwa im Fall Rauch. Hier reicht die Palette von Landmaschinen über Fruchtsaftgetränke bis zu verschiedenen Mehlsorten aus Österreich. Egal, alles Originale! Andersherum: An wen soll man bei den Richter

veloped by a cousin of Joseph Beuys. The concept artist Hanne Darboven is a descendant of the founders of the Hamburg coffee dynasty of the same name. The sculptor Vera Röhm is a descendant of the founders of Röhm Plexiglas. Picasso perfume is a brand owned by Picasso's daughter Paloma. Niki de St. Phalle created her own line of products.

Difficult decisions have to be made when one discovers different products with the same famous artist's name, such as Rauch, for instance. Products that go by this name range from agricultural machines to fruit juices and various types of flour from Austria. All originals! Conversely, who are we to associate with Richter Fire Rolls? Ludwig Richter, the 19th century illustrator or Gerhard Richter, the chameleon of contemporary art? And who are we to associate with Merz Special Dragées?

Fontana Chymos Anana, 2004
Ananas-Saft, 1 l
19,9 x 10,3 x 6,5 cm

Fontana Chymos Anana, 2004
Pineapple juice, 1 l
19.9 x 10.3 x 6.5 cm

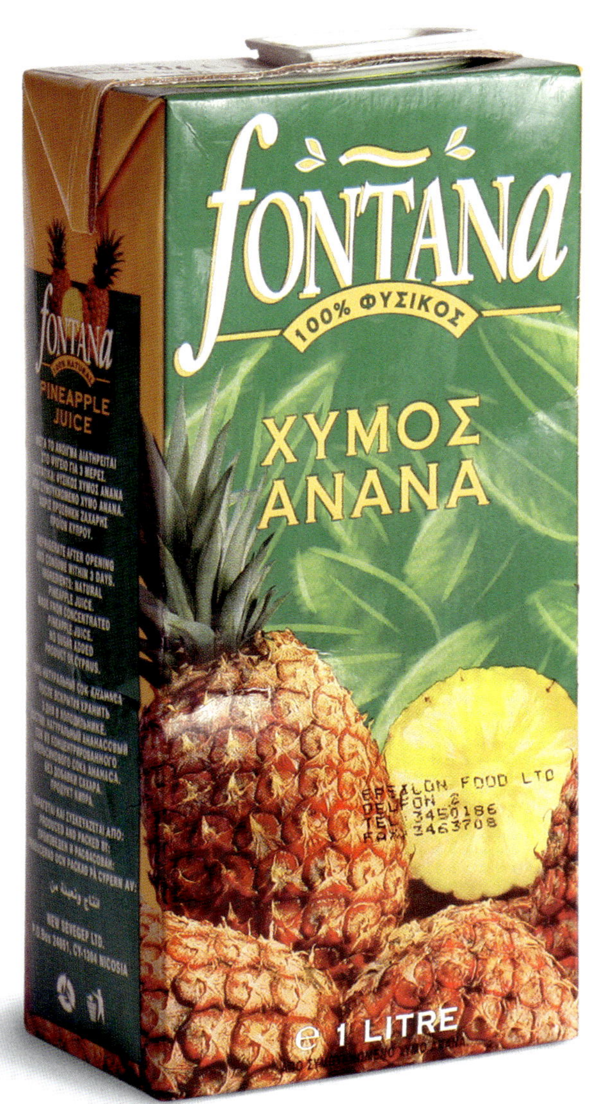
fonTana
100% ΦΥΣΙΚΟΣ
ΧΥΜΟΣ
ΑΝΑΝΑ
fonTana
100% NATURAL
PINEAPPLE
JUICE
e 1 LITRE

Feuerröllchen denken? An Ludwig Richter, den Illustrator des 19. Jahrhunderts, oder an Gerhard Richter, das Chamäleon der Gegenwartskunst? An wen angesichts der Merz Spezial Dragees: Mario oder Gerhard Merz? Geradezu problematisch wird es bei Stella: auf zwei Produkte – Hartweizengrieß aus Griechenland und die erwähnten Schweizer Butterkekse – kommen drei Künstler: Jacques (Barock), Joseph (Futurismus) und Frank Stella (Hard Edge).

Auch kategoriale Zuordnungen erweisen sich mitunter als schwierig, etwa, wenn ein Familienbetrieb von einem größeren Konsortium aufgekauft wurde: Appel zum Beispiel gehört jetzt Richter. Gaudì macht Reklame auf Fußballtrikots von Lotto. Interessant auch die folgenden Sonderfälle. So ließ sich der Inhaber der Michelin Besteckfabrik aus Krefeld vom eigenen

Mario or Gerhard Merz? In the case of Stella, things become really problematic. Here, we have three artists, including Jacques (Baroque), Joseph (Futurism) and Frank Stella (Hard Edge), vying for association with two products, including Greek durum wheat semolina and the Swiss butter cookies mentioned above.

Classifications can also prove difficult when a family-operated business has been acquired by a large corporation. Appel, for instance, now belongs to Richter. Gaudì advertises its products on Lotto soccer jerseys. Then there are the following special cases. The owner of the Michelin cutlery factory in Krefeld, Germany used his own last name of Michelangelo as a source of inspiration for a Michelangelo line of products. The name of the Manet motor scooter comes from the Manin Mountains

Fragonard, 2007

Rosenseife

3 x 8,8 x 5,9 cm

Fragonard, 2007

Rose soap

3 x 8.8 x 5.9 cm

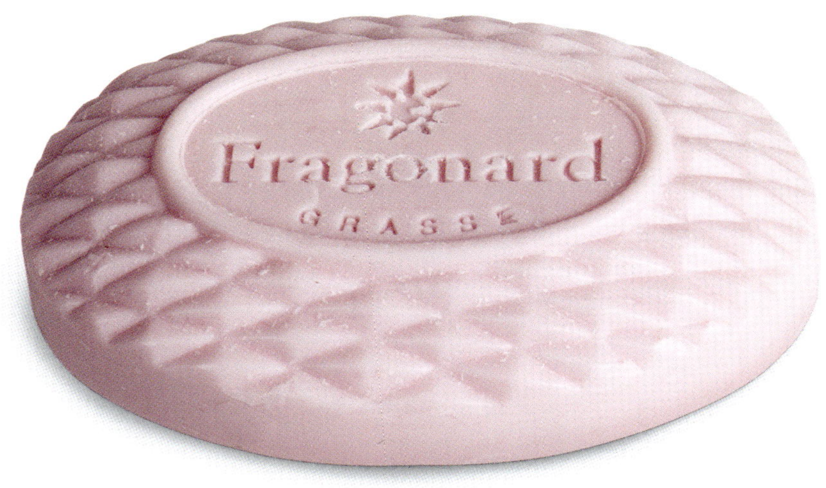

Nachnamen zur Produktserie Michelangelo inspirieren. Der Manet-Motorroller verdankt seinen Namen den Manin-Bergen in der Umgebung des Werks. Die Vermeer Manufacturing Company unterhält ein Vermeer Museum im US-Staat Iowa. Die Lebensmittel von Newman's Own erinnern nicht nur an den Maler Barnett Newman, sondern werden von einem Künstler aus einer anderen Sparte produziert, dem Filmschauspieler Paul Newman (der alle Erlöse für wohltätige Zwecke spendet). Verkehrte Welt: Künstler nehmen Produktnamen an. So änderten der in Dessau geborene Wolf Knoebel und sein Freund Rainer Giese, beide Beuys-Schüler an der Düsseldorfer Akademie, ihre Vornamen in IMI, nach dem Putzmittel aus der DDR: »IMI gegen groben Schmutz«.

near the factory. The Vermeer Manufacturing Company operates a Vermeer museum in the U.S. state of Iowa. The food products sold under the Newman's Own label not only point to the painter Barnett Newman, they are actually produced by an artist from a different branch, namely, the actor Paul Newman (who donates all proceeds to charity). And what a world we live in when artists go as far as to adopt product names! For instance, Wolf Knoebel, a native of Dessau, Germany, and his friend Rainer Giese, both students of Beuys at the Düsseldorfer Akademie, changed their first names to IMI in keeping with a cleaning agent manufactured in the former GDR: "IMI tackles serious dirt."

Fuchs, 1999
Fisch Würzer, 80 g
Höhe 12 cm, ø 4,3 cm

Fuchs, 1999
Fish Spice, 80 g
height: 12 cm, ø 4.3 cm

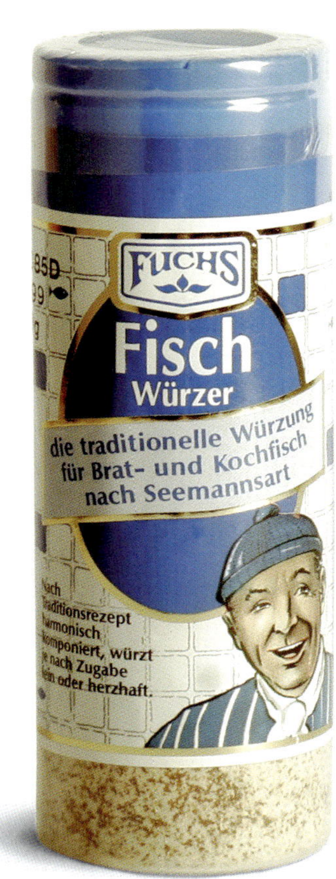
FUCHS
Fisch
Würzer
die traditionelle Würzung
für Brat- und Kochfisch
nach Seemannsart
Nach
Traditionsrezept
harmonisch
komponiert, würzt
je nach Zugabe
fein oder herzhaft.

Dass die gezielte Benennung von Produkten nach Künstlern – und nur selten nach Künstlerinnen – eine Marketing-Maßnahme darstellt, liegt auf der Hand. Doch welche Namen müssen bevorzugt herhalten, was verbindet sich mit ihnen? Beginnen wir mit einem ungewöhnlichen Beispiel: dem Weingut Duchamp in Kalifornien. Die Namensgebung gehe, wie mir Pat Lenz, Winzerin und selbst Bildhauerin, erklärt, auf ihre Hassliebe zu Duchamp zurück, der mit seinem Kunstgriff, einen vorgefertigten Gegenstand in einen Ausstellungsraum zu überführen, die Konzept- und die Objektkunst gleichzeitig begründet hat. Ich beschließe, alle Stücke meiner Sammlung mit einem ArtBrand-Stempel zu versehen, auch den Duchamp.

Die meisten Unternehmen greifen zu den Namen der bekannten Meister, wenn auch nicht immer aus nahe liegenden

Giving products the names of famous artists—seldom the names of famous female artists—is an obvious marketing device. But what names are the most promising and what is associated with them? Let's begin with an unusual example: the Duchamp winery in California. As Pat Lenz, herself a vintner and sculptor, explained to me, the naming goes back to her love-hate relationship to Duchamp who simultaneously founded concept and object art by transporting prefabricated objects to galleries and dubbing them art. I have resolved to furnish all of the pieces in my collection with an ArtBrand imprint, including the Duchamp.

Most companies give their products the names of famous masters—even if the rationale for doing so isn't quite so obvious—as in the case of the Syrom Company in Vinci, Italy

Giotto Stick, 2005
Klebestift
Höhe 10,1 cm, ⌀ 2,6 cm

Giotto Stick, 2005
Glue stick
height: 10.1 cm, ⌀ 2.6 cm

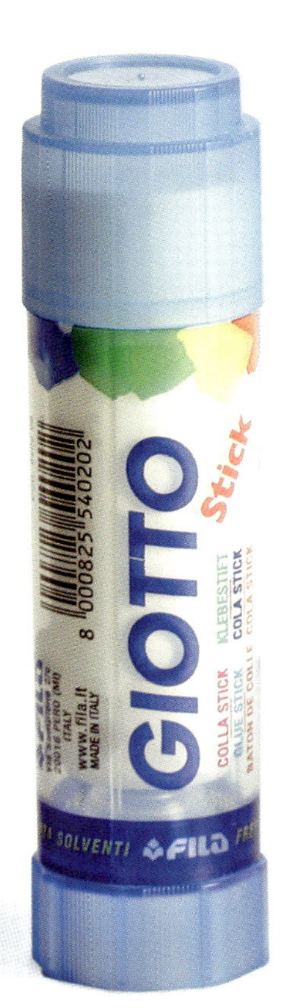

GIOTTO
Stick
COLLA STICK
GLUE STICK
BATON DE COLLE
COLA STICK
KLEBESTIFT
FILA
SOLVENTI
MADE IN ITALY
www.fila.it
ITALY
8 0008251540202

Gründen, wie im Fall der Firma Syrom, die aus Vinci stammt und ein Leonardo-Klebeband anfertigt. Die alten Namen sind rechtlich nicht mehr geschützt: Das Copyright, auf das auch die Erben Anspruch haben, währt laut »Berner Übereinkunft« 50 Jahre, in den USA und den Ländern der Europäischen Union 70 Jahre, gerechnet ab dem Hinscheiden des Urhebers. Benennungen nach jüngeren Künstlern sind also nicht ohne weiteres möglich. Fehlt dem Miro-Parfüm, dessen Flacon-Design an den Stil des katalanischen Künstlers angelehnt ist, deshalb der Apostroph über dem o? Ein Lokal an der Kunsthalle Mannheim trug früher einmal den Namen Picasso, bis dessen Nachkommen ein Veto einlegten. Seit 1994 heißt es Picco. Dennoch sind viele Restaurants weiterhin nach Picasso benannt, sogar ein Friseursalon (in Sachsen-Anhalt) – im

that produces rolls of tape called Leonardo. The old names are no longer protected by copyright. According to the "Bern Convention," copyrights apply for a period of 50 years (the period is 70 years in the United States and the countries of the European Union) from the date of the originator's death. This effectively rules out using the names of younger artists, i.e. unless one first obtains formal consent. Is this perhaps the reason why Miro perfume, whose flacon design is reminiscent of the Catalonian artist's style, does without the accent? A restaurant attached to the Kunsthalle Mannheim used to be called Picasso until Picasso's descendants objected. Since 1994, the name of the restaurant has been Picco. But there are obviously many restaurants that are still called Picasso. I have even come across a hairdresser's named Picasso. Con-

Goya, 1998
Wiener Würstchen, 142 g
Höhe 6,2 cm, ⌀ 6,3 cm.

Goya, 1998
Vienna Sausage, 142 g
height: 6.2 cm, ⌀ 6.3 cm.

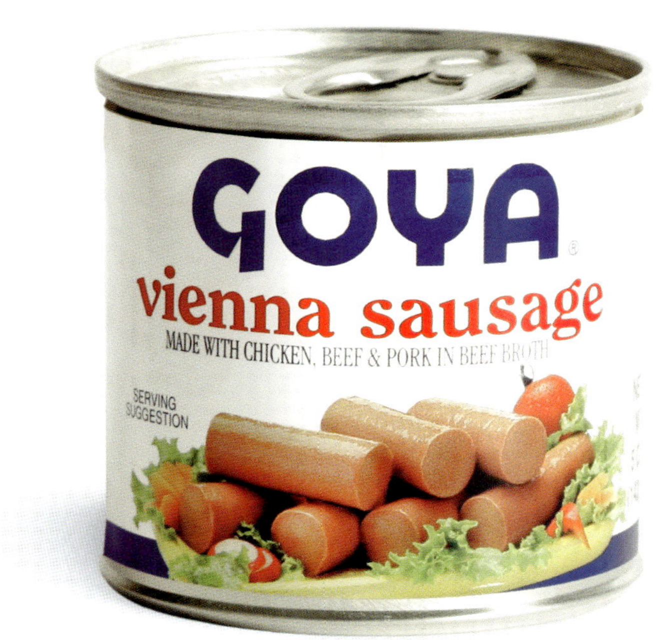

GOYA
vienna sausage
MADE WITH CHICKEN, BEEF & PORK IN BEEF BROTH
SERVING
SUGGESTION

Gegensatz zum Citroën C4 Picasso vermutlich unautorisiert. Hinzu kommen zahllose Cafés, Bars, Hotels und Schiffe mit weiteren Künstlernamen. Leonardo, Michelangelo und Tiepolo verkehren sogar als Züge zwischen Deutschland und Italien.

Für die Zeit der italienischen Renaissance, die den »Divino artista« hervorgebracht hat, den göttlichen Künstler, können keine Ansprüche mehr geltend gemacht werden. Hier gibt es auch so viele bekannte Namen, dass sich ganze Produktreihen daraus bilden lassen. So benennt die Firma OZ eine Serie von Leichtmetallfelgen nach Botticelli, Giotto, Leonardo, Michelangelo, Palladio und Raffaello, ergänzt durch den Klassizisten Canova. Wir finden dieselben Renaissancekünstler bei LED, einem italienischen Hersteller von medizinischen Apparaten, der seine Reihe der »Grandi maestri« noch um Donatello,

trary to the Citroën C4 Picasso, the use of Picasso by these establishments is presumably unauthorized, not to mention the countless cafés, bars, hotels and ships named after artists. There are even trains by the name of Leonardo, Michelangelo, and Tiepolo that run between Germany and Italy.

Copyright claims no longer apply to the time of the Italian Renaissance, which gave rise to the "divino artista," the divine artist. Here, there are enough famous names to account for entire product lines. The OZ Company, for instance, names the products in its series of light alloy rims after Botticelli, Giotto, Leonardo, Michelangelo, Palladio, and Raffaello. And for good measure, OZ adds the classical Canova. We find the same Renaissance artists at LED, an Italian manufacturer of medical devices. LED goes a step further by naming the devices in its

Horn, 1968
Brautkleid, japanischer Stil
Größe 38

Horn, 1968
Wedding Dress, japanese style
size: 8

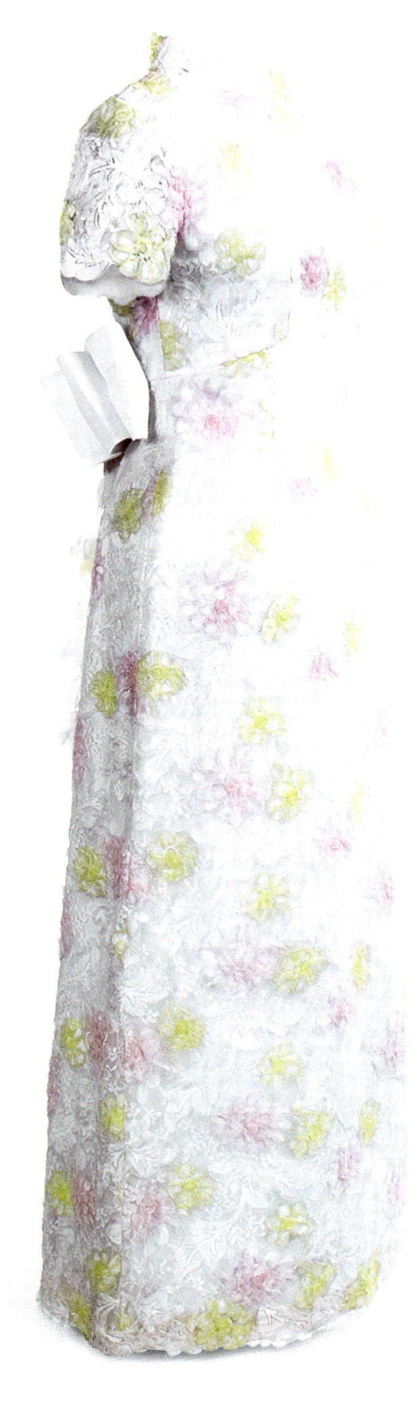

Canaletto, Tintoretto, Caravaggio und Bernini erweitert, also auch die Zeit des Barock berücksichtigt. Bis auf die Schaltknöpfe sehen sie alle gleich aus. Derselben Namen bedienen sich auch der italienische Bio-Hausbauer Cecamore Costruzioni und die Firma Tuscany, die Ledertaschen herstellt.

Den Rekord hält das Unternehmen SIB, das Zäune und Tore in Frankreich produziert und in seiner »Serie Evolution« Gartentore anbietet, die vorrangig nach französischen Künstlern benannt sind, in alphabetischer Reihenfolge: Bazille, Braque, Cézanne, Chardin, Corot, Courbet, Degas, Delacroix, Denis, Dufy, Gauguin, Ingres, La Tour, Matisse, Millet, Monet, Poussin, Renoir, Signac, Sisley und Vlaminck. Der Schwerpunkt liegt auf dem 19. Jahrhundert. Ging hier ein Besuch des Musée d'Orsay voraus? Da die bekannten Namen dort offensicht-

"grandi maestri" line after Donatello, Canaletto, Tintoretto, Caravaggio, and Bernini so as to also account for the Baroque period. Except for the control buttons, the devices all look the same. The very same names are also used by Cecamore Costruzioni, an Italy-based builder of environmentally-friendly homes, and the Tuscany Company, which makes leather bags.

The record, however, seems to be held by the SIB Company, which manufactures fences and gates in France. SIB offers garden gates in its "Serie Evolution" that are primarily named after French artists, including Bazille, Braque, Cézanne, Chardin, Corot, Courbet, Degas, Delacroix, Denis, Dufy, Gauguin, Ingres, La Tour, Matisse, Millet, Monet, Poussin, Renoir, Signac, Sisley, and Vlaminck. Here, the focus is on the 19th century, and one is inclined to suspect that the summary decision

Kandinsky Premiums & Promotions, 2007
Schlüsselanhänger
1 x 9,4 x 2,8 cm

Kandinsky Premiums & Promotions, 2007
Key chain
1 x 9.4 x 2.8 cm

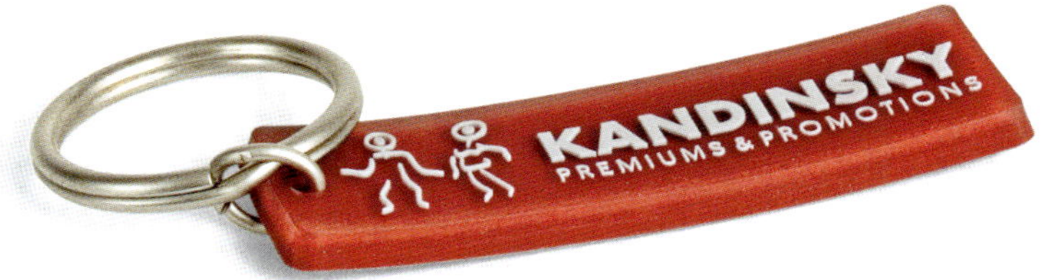

lich für die »Evolution« nicht ausreichten, wurden auch der Louvre und Künstler aus anderen Ländern und Zeiten bemüht: Bellotto, Botticelli, Cassatt, Canaletto, Dalí, Giotto, Goya, da Vinci, Miró, Picasso, Reynolds, Turner und Vasarely.

Schauen wir uns einen schon mehrfach erwähnten Namen näher an: Giotto. So hieß auch die ESA-Raumsonde, die sich 1986 dem Kometen Halley bis auf 596 km näherte. Die Namenswahl ist begründet, denn Giotto hatte den alle 76 Jahre wiederkehrenden Kometen 1301 selbst gesehen und in seinem Fresko »Anbetung der Könige« gemalt. Nachvollziehbar ist daher auch die Benennung einer Public Domain Software nach Giotto, die speziell der Videoastronomie dient. Doch was hat es mit der Software Giotto MobilCAD für die Wohnungseinrichtung auf sich? Dient der technische Aspekt als Legiti-

behind these names was preceded by a visit to the Musée d'Orsay. But then it turns out that these famous names were apparently not enough to account for the "Evolution," so the company goes on to enlist artists exhibited at the Louvre and even artists from other countries and periods, including Bellotto, Botticelli, Cassatt, Canaletto, Dalí, Giotto, Goya, da Vinci, Miró, Picasso, Reynolds, Turner, and Vasarely.

Let's take a closer look at the above-mentioned name of Giotto. Giotto was also the name of the ESA spacecraft that came within 596 kilometers of Halley's Comet in 1986. The name chosen for the spacecraft is especially apt in light of the fact that Giotto himself is thought to have seen the comet, which reappears every 76 years, in 1301 and painted an image of it in his nativity fresco "Adoration of the Magi." The

Kauffmann Pikantes Allerlei, 2001
Feinsaures Essiggemüse, 670 g
Höhe 13,7 cm, ø 9,6 cm

Kauffmann Pikantes Allerlei, 2001
Pickled vegetables, 670 g
height: 13.7 cm, ø 9.6 cm

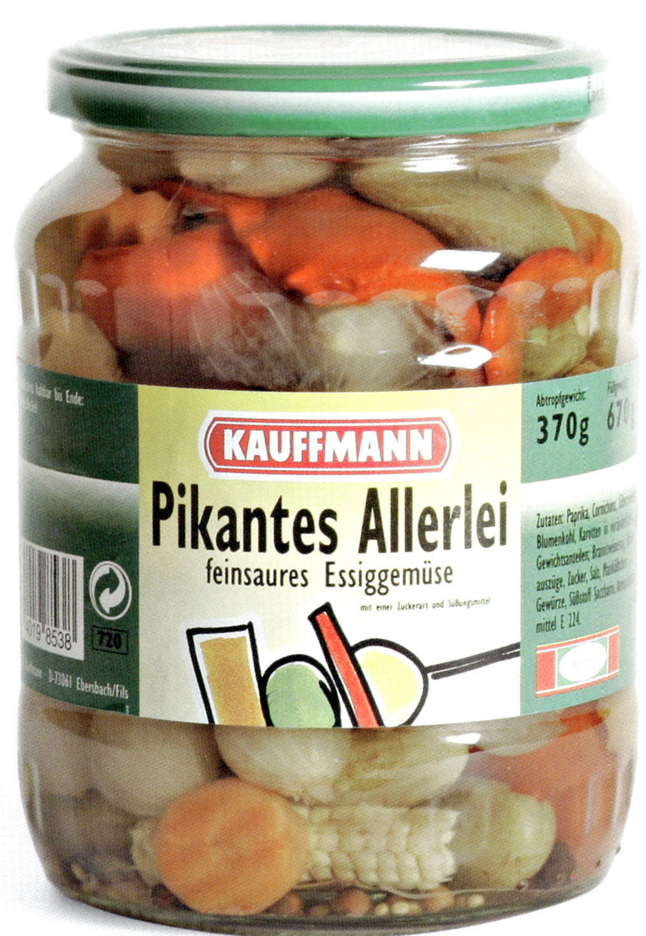

KAUFFMANN
Pikantes Allerlei
feinsaures Essiggemüse
mit einer Zuckerart und Süßungsmittel
Abtropfgewicht: 370g
Füllgewicht: 670 g
Zutaten: Paprika, Cornichons, Silberzwiebeln, Blumenkohl, Karotten in veränderlichen Gewichtsanteilen; Branntweinessig, Branntweinauszüge, Zucker, Salz, Pflanzenöl, Gewürze, Süßstoff Saccharin, Konservierungsmittel E 224.
720
Ebersbach/Fils

mation? Soll der Name Giotto zeigen, dass das Produkt »state of the art« ist, die derzeit bestmögliche Ausführung?

Dann trifft dies auch für das Mammografik-Gerät Giotto Image der amerikanischen Progressive Medical Corporation zu, den elektronischen Kartenleseapparat Giotto aus Argentinien, ebenso wie für das Faxgerät Giotto Laser der Telecom Italia, eine Giotto-Kaffeemaschine der Espresso Company Milano, die Giotto-Armbanduhren der Firma TBbuti, den Rollschuh Giotto von Roll Line TM oder die Verpackungsstraße Giotto von tecnopacking (offensichtlich ein Prozesskunstwerk). Mit den Fotostativen der Giotto's Group aus Taipeh, China, und der Membranpumpe Giotto Airless für Spritzpistolen von Larius lässt sich sogar Kunst machen. (Ist es notwendig zu erwähnen, dass zahllose Farben und Utensilien aus dem Künstlerbedarfs-geschäft nach großen Meistern benannt sind?)

naming of a public domain software that is used to support video astronomy after Giotto is also plausible. But what is the explanation behind the software Giotto MobilCAD for interior decorating? Is it enough when a product has a technical as-pect? Is the name Giotto supposed to signify that the product represents the state of the art?

If so, then this will apply as well to the Giotto Image mam-mography device manufactured by the U.S.-based Progres-sive Medical Corporation, the Giotto electronic card scanner from Argentina, the Giotto laser fax machine by Telecom Italy, the Giotto coffee machine by the Milano Espresso Company, the Giotto wrist watch by the TBbuti Company, the Giotto roller skate by Roll Line TM, and the Giotto packaging line by tecnopacking (apparently a case of process art). One can even use the camera tripods made by the Giotto's Group of Taiwan

Kiefer, 2007
Roggenmischbrot, 500 g
ca. 20 x 18 x 12 cm

Kiefer, 2007
Mixed Rye Bread, 500 g
c. 20 x 18 x 12 cm

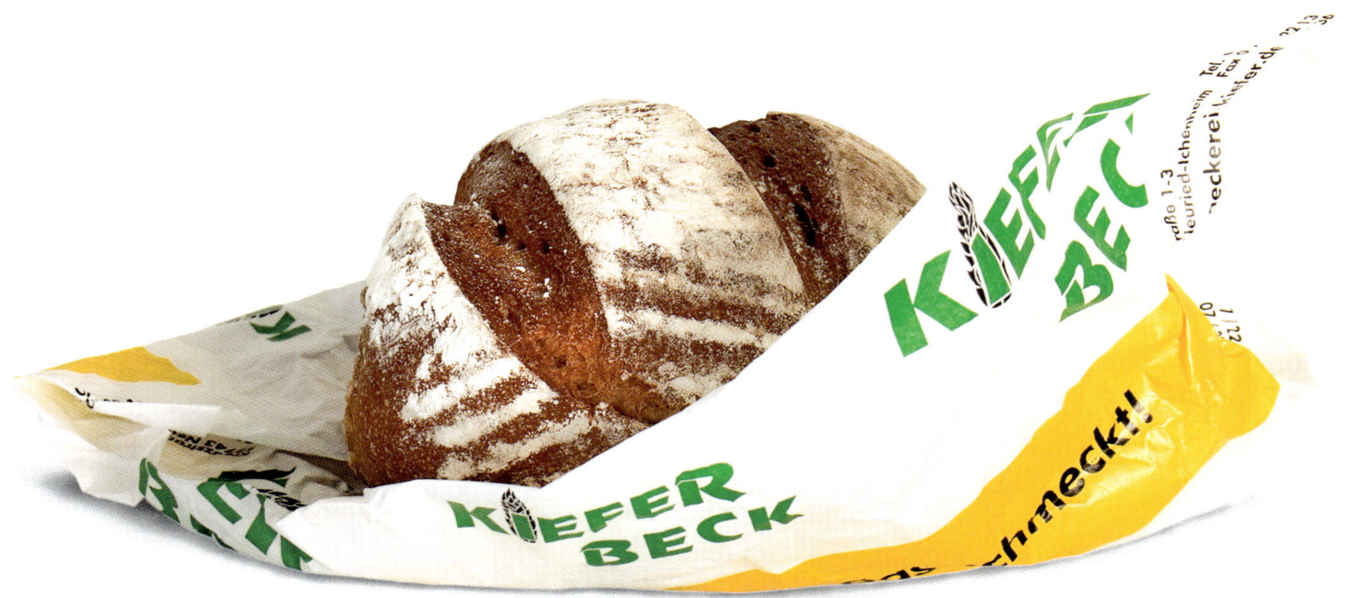

KIEFER BECK
KIEFER BECK

Entlegener scheinen dagegen die Balkongeländer Giotto der Vettaflex s.r.l., die Wohnzimmertische Collezione Giotto von Vetraria Vismara, der Pellets-Einbaukamin Giotto von SiCalor, die Pfannen- und Topflinie Giotto von Bialetti, der Rucksack Giotto von Benetton, der Rahmenpfosten Giotto für Plakatständer der Inntec Werbung, die bioaktive Matratze Giotto plus von Mobles Godia, die schottische Wolle Giotto von Colinette Yarn (auch im Farbton Cézanne erhältlich) oder die 600 ml-Nagertränke Giotto für Hamster und Mäuse von Nagerplanet.

Die meisten Produkte mit dem Namen Giotto stammen aus Italien oder Spanien. Dennoch gibt es in Italien kein Giotto-Konfekt wie in Deutschland. Hat Ferrero im Heimatland zu viel

and the Giotto diaphragm-pump airless paint sprayer by Larius to make art. It probably goes without saying that numerous paints and other art supplies have been named after great masters.

In contrast, the following products come across as rather remote from the artist: the Giotto balcony railings by Vettaflex s.r.l., the Giotto living room table collection by Vetraria Vismara, the Giotto built-in pellet stove by SiCalor, the Giotto kitchenware line by Bialetti, the Giotto backpack by Benetton, the Giotto poster frames by Inntec Werbung, the Giotto Plus bio-active mattress by Mobles Godia, the Giotto Scottish wool by Colinette Yarn (also available in the color Cézanne) and the 600-ml Giotto trough for hamsters and mice by Nagerplanet.

Klein Q-ELITE XV, 2008
Rennrad, Spezialanfertigung mit Karbonrahmen
in International Klein Blue
ca. 100 x 45 x 166 cm

Klein Q-ELITE XV, 2008
Custom racing bike with carbon frame
in International Klein Blue
c. 100 x 45 x 166 cm

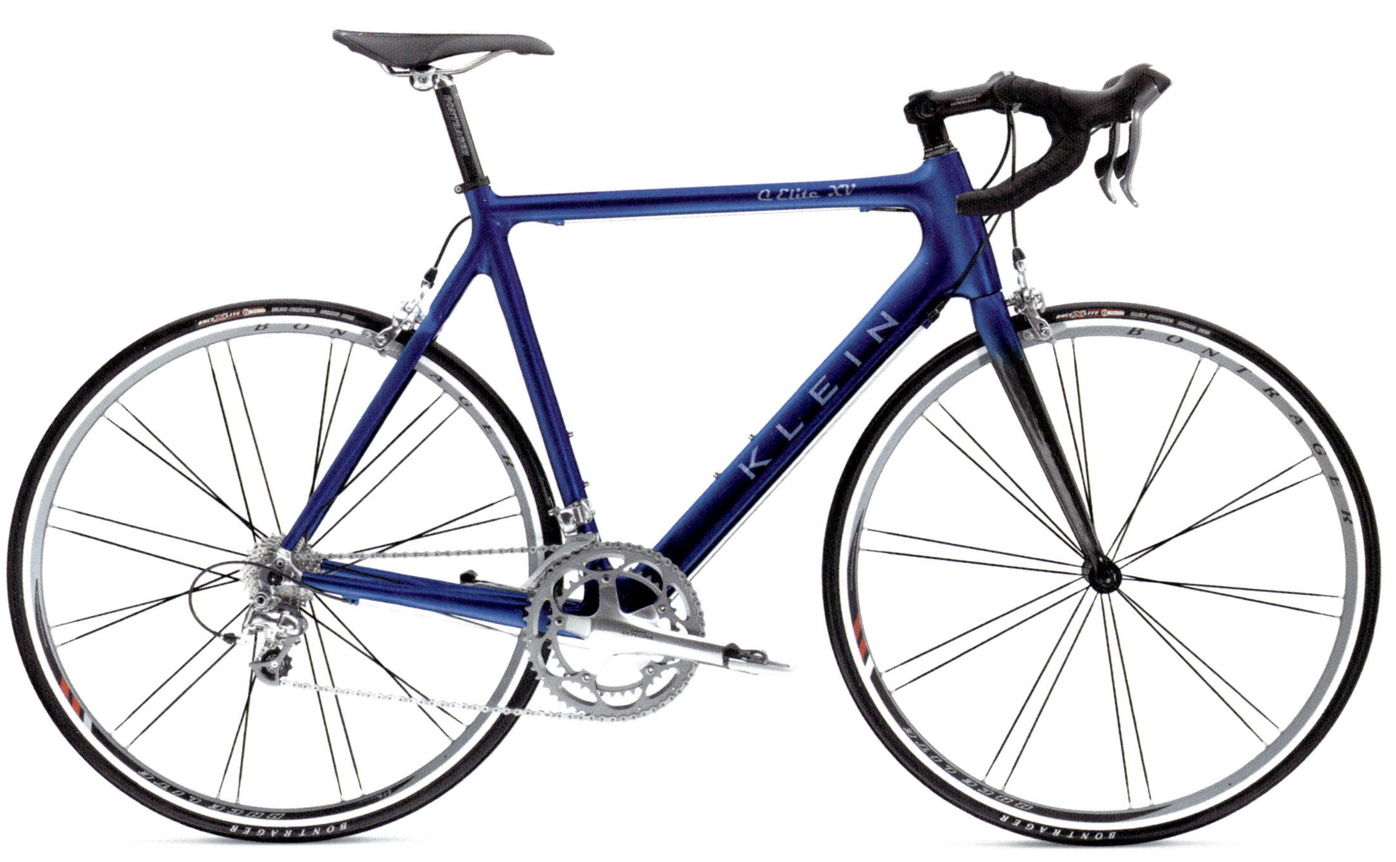

Q Elite XV
KLEIN

Konkurrenz ausfindig gemacht? Dort firmiert auch ein weit verbreitetes Schreibwarensortiment von Fila unter dem Namen Giotto, darunter Filzstifte, Pinsel und Marker. Offensichtlich gibt es für Künstlernamen kein Monopol; die Strategie geht aber nur auf, wenn nicht zu viele Unternehmen das Gleiche im selben Marktsegment oder in enger geografischer Nachbarschaft tun.

Wenn dennoch so viele Hersteller ihre Produkte nach dem Wegbereiter der Renaissance benennen, liegt dies nicht am kostbaren Gold in den Giotto-Gemälden, auch nicht an der Fragilität seiner Fresken. Da seit dem Beginn der Neuzeit weniger die manuelle Fertigkeit als die geistige Leistung von Bedeutung ist, geht es letztlich um die abstrakten Qualitäten, um Kreativität und Innovationskraft, die großen Künstlern zu

While most of the products named Giotto come from Italy and Spain, there is no Giotto confectionery—of the sort one finds in every supermarket in Germany—on the manufacturer's domestic market. Did the Ferrero Company determine that a certain degree of market saturation had already been reached? Italy is also home to a popular line of Giotto stationery supplies by Fila, including felt-tip pens, paint brushes and markers. Given the apparent lack of exclusive rights to the names of famous artists, the strategy of using such names will only succeed if not too many other companies do the same, or do the same in the same market segment or within a relatively small geographic area.

If so many manufacturers decide nonetheless to name their products after the pioneers of the Renaissance, the reason is

Leonardo Transparente, 2004
60 m Klebeband
Verpackung 16,1 x 11,6 x 2 cm

Leonardo Transparente, 2004
60 m roll of tape
package size: 16.1 x 11.6 x 2 cm

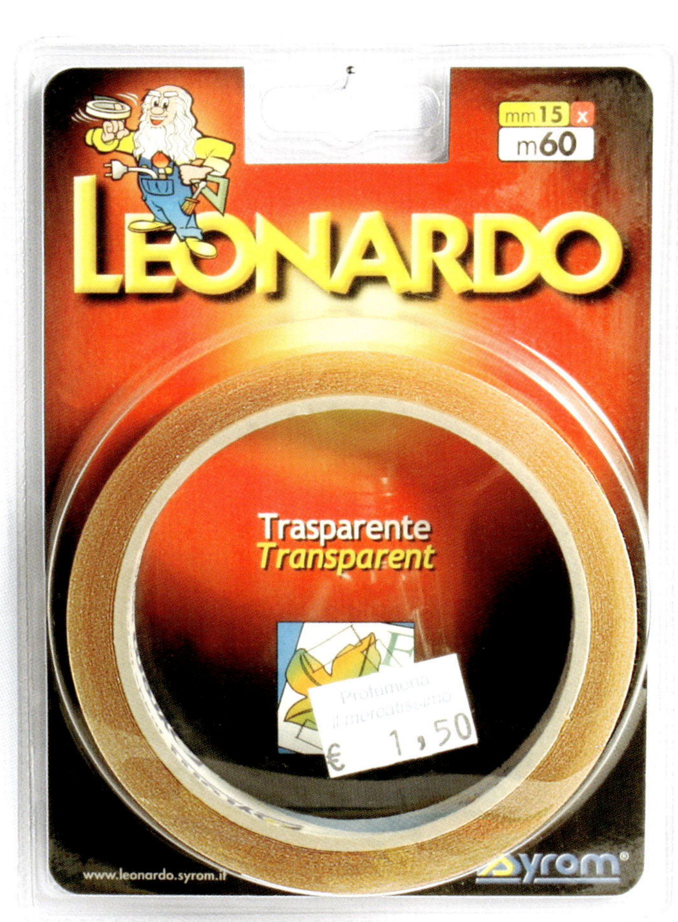

LEONARDO
mm15 x
m60
Trasparente
Transparent
€ 1,50
www.leonardo.syrom.it
Syrom

eigen sind. Es gibt eine Ökonomie der symbolischen Werte, die sich auf die Waren übertragen lässt. Je wegweisender die künstlerische Erneuerung, je verbreiteter das gleichnamige Produkt, desto mehr Menschen können daran teilhaben, frei nach René Descartes: Consumo, ergo sum artista. ∎

Literaturhinweise | Further Reading
Sandra Danicke: Giotto. In: Frankfurter Rundschau, 14.11.1998.
Beate Passow/Boris von Brauchitsch: kunst und konsum.
In: Frankfurter Rundschau Magazin, Juli 2000.
Beate Passow/Boris von Brauchitsch: Künstlerporträts. Frankfurt 2001.

not the precious gold in Giotto paintings or the fragility of his frescos. In light of the fact that the significance of mental capacity (or evidence thereof) has surpassed that of pure manual skill since the beginning of the modern age, it is ultimately a matter of the abstract qualities, creativity and innovation that are exhibited by great artists. Symbolic values have an economic aspect that allows them to be transferred to common products. The more pioneering the artistic renewal, the more widespread the product of the same name, the greater the opportunity people will have to experience these values. To adapt Descartes' existential conclusion: consumo, ergo sum artista. ∎

Lichtenstein, 2007
Vitamin B 12, 1 ml Injektionslösung
Höhe 4,8 cm, ø 1,1 cm

Lichtenstein, 2007
Vitamin B 12, injection solution, 1 ml
height: 4.8 cm, ø 1.1 cm

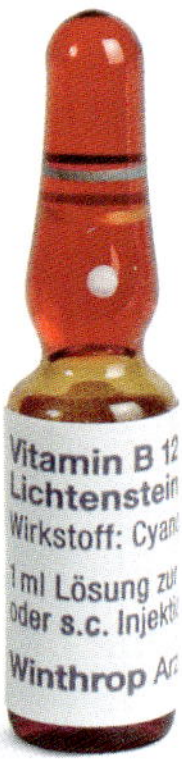

Vitamin B 12
Lichtenstein
Wirkstoff: Cyan
1 ml Lösung zu
oder s.c. Injekt
Winthrop Ar

Angelika Epple

Kunst, Konsum, Kommerz und das Auge des Betrachters | Art, Business, Consumption, and the Eye of the Beholder

Massenkonsum, so eine weit verbreitete Überzeugung, führt zu einer Profanierung von Kunst und Künstlern. Walter Benjamin hat dieser kulturkritischen Haltung in seinem Essay über »Das Kunstwerk im Zeitalter seiner technischen Reproduzierbarkeit«[1] ihren klassischen Ausdruck verliehen. Heute hat die Realität Benjamins schlimmste Befürchtungen überholt: Picassobecher, Miróteller, Tischskulpturen von Niki de Saint Phalle – es gibt kein Entkommen vor einer »auralos« gewordenen Kunst. Wenn wir mit den hier gezeigten »ArtBrands« nun Produkten im Museum begegnen, haben sie dann das letzte Bollwerk zur Verteidigung der Kunst gegen ihren Warencharakter erobert?

Many have suggested that mass consumption will ultimately diminish the significance of art and artists. In his essay "The Work of Art in the Age of Mechanical Reproduction"[1], Walter Benjamin provided a compelling and influential account of such cultural misgivings. Today, just over 70 years after the publication of his essay, the settings of our day-to-day lives seem to offer dramatic confirmation of Benjamin's premonition. We see Picasso cups, Miró plates, and table-top sculptures by Niki de Saint Phalle. Indeed, there is no escape from works of art that have been divested of their "aura." And now there is "ArtBrands", a museum exhibition that promises us an encounter with ordinary products. Has one of the last bastions of hope against the advancing commercialization of art been conquered?

Lotto Go Centrale 2000
Fußballschuhe
Größe 42, je 13 x 28 x 9,8 cm

Lotto Go Centrale 2000
Football shoes
size: 8.5, 13 x 28 x 9.8 cm

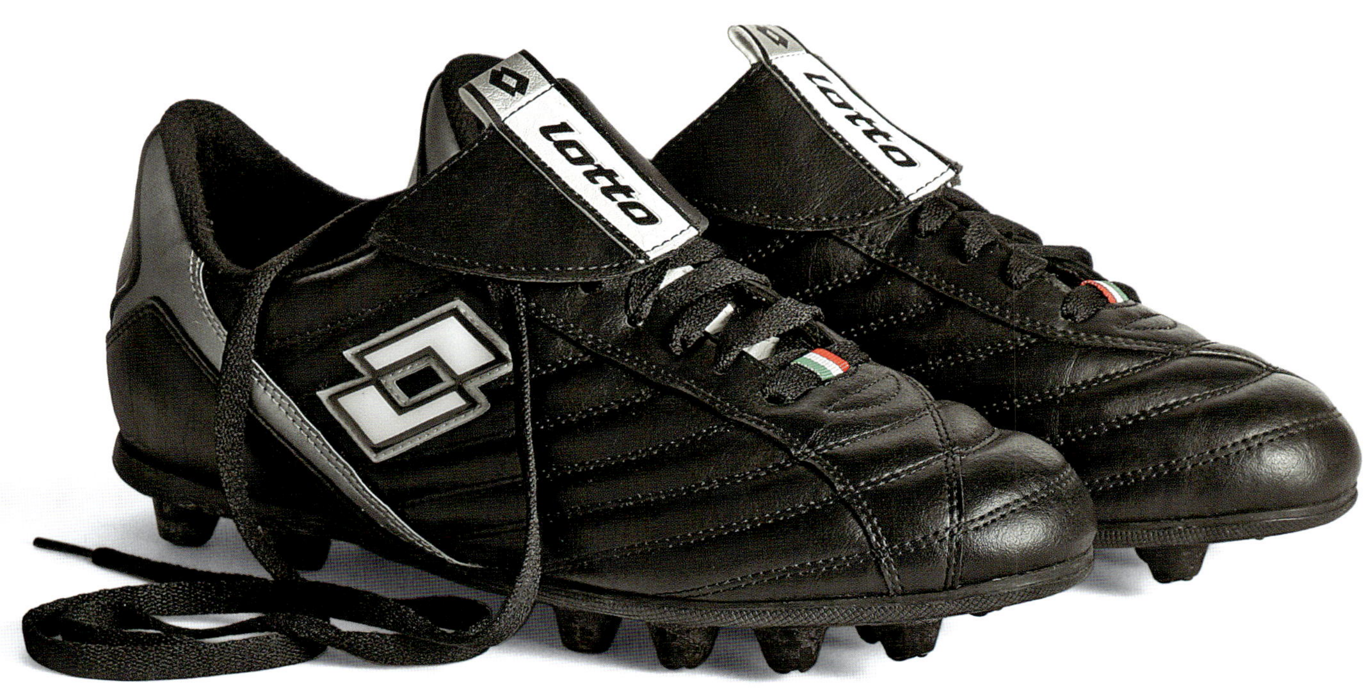

Gönnen wir uns einen Blick in die Geschichte einer Beziehung. Kunst, Konsum, Kommerz sind, historisch gesehen, ein dreihundert Jahre altes Gespann. Die Entstehung des Konsums als einer der Hauptcharakteristika heutiger Gesellschaften lässt sich auf zahlreiche historische Entwicklungen zurückführen: Damit man von Konsum im heutigen Sinn des Wortes sprechen kann, musste sich zunächst eine neue, mittlere Kategorie von Waren entwickeln.[2] Sie grenzte sich einerseits von reinen Luxusprodukten wie Kaffee, Schokolade, Gewürzen usw. ab, die ausschließlich den Eliten vorbehalten waren. Andererseits unterschied sie sich auch von Gütern, die das reine Überleben sicherten und auf alltäglichen Bedarf orientiert waren. In dem Maße, in dem sich eine ständische Ordnung auflöste, gewannen andere soziale Distinktions-

Before sounding the alarm, let's take a look at the history of a long relationship. Art, consumption, and business have been in cahoots for around 300 years. The steady rise of consumption as one of the main characteristics of contemporary society can be traced to numerous historical developments.[2] Consumption as we know it today has its historical origin in the introduction of a new class of product that was positioned between luxury items such as coffee, chocolate, and spices, which were reserved for the privileged class, and the staples of life, i.e. those day-to-day products people needed to secure their very existence. As traditional class structures begin to erode, other features of distinction will emerge to take their place. Consumption and consumer behavior, for instance, have proven very well-suited in this regard. Histori-

Manet S 100, 1960
Motorroller
150 x 196 x 56,5 cm

Manet S 100, 1960
Scooter
150 x 196 x 56.5 cm

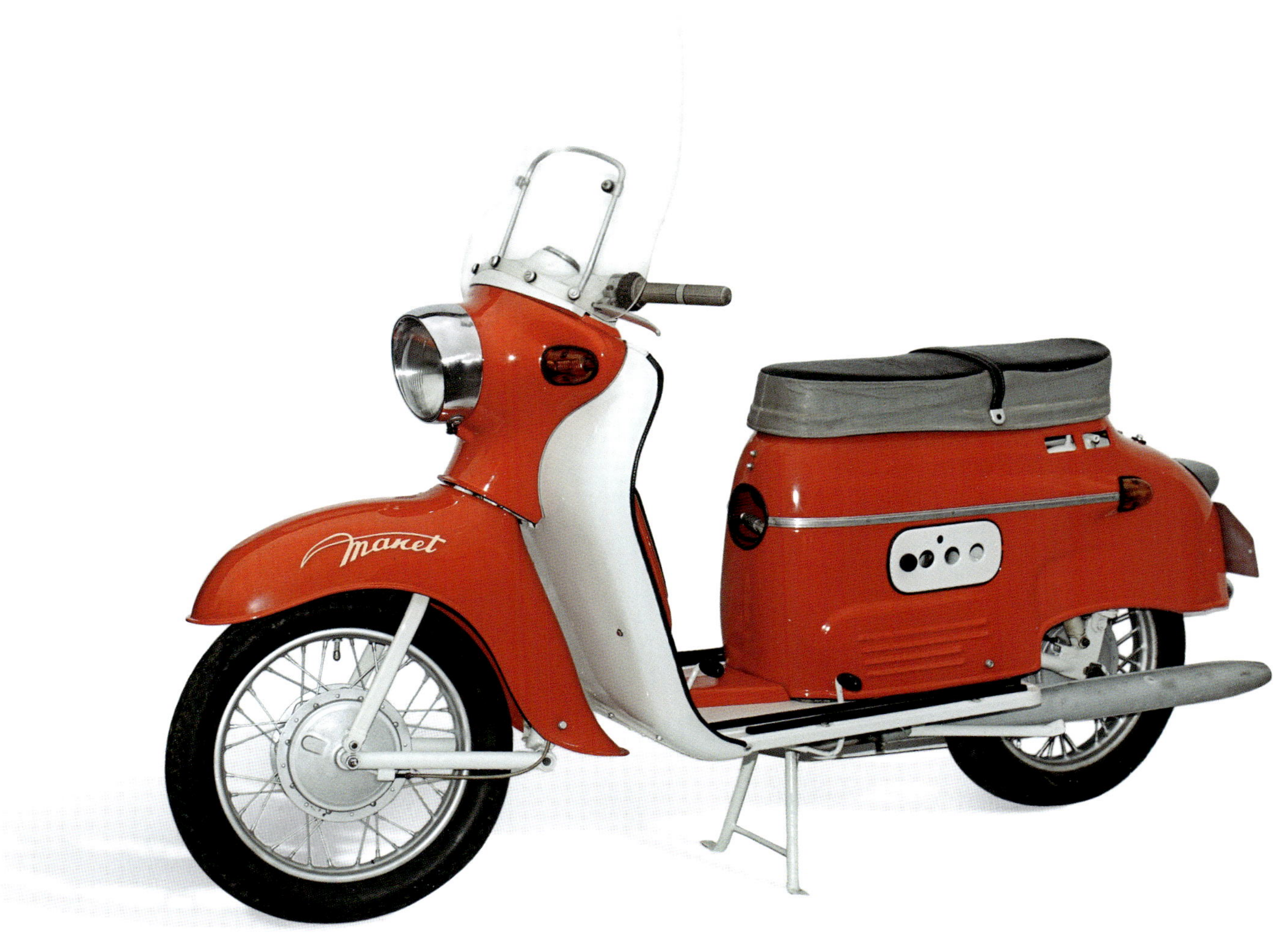
Manet

merkmale an Bedeutung. Konsum und Konsummuster eignen sich hierfür bis heute in besonderem Maße. Es musste sich aber auch die gesellschaftliche Erwerbsstruktur ändern, damit überhaupt finanzielle Ressourcen vorhanden waren, die in Konsum investiert werden konnten. Luxusprodukte mussten durch neue Produktionsformen, durch die Revolution des Transportwesens billiger werden, damit sie von mehr Menschen gekauft werden konnten. Hier wären noch zahlreiche weitere Entwicklungen zu nennen,[3] ich möchte mich jedoch auf eine konzentrieren, die in unserem Zusammenhang von besonderem Interesse ist. In den Niederlanden des 17. Jahrhunderts entwickelte sich erstmals ein Kunstmarkt, der noch ganz von der konkreten Bedeutung eines Marktes zur Deckung des alltäglichen Bedarfs gekennzeich-

cally speaking, however, certain established rules governing the transaction of goods also had to change in order allow for the broader availability of financial resources that was necessary to enable and drive consumption. Furthermore, luxury products had to be made more affordable via new forms of production and transport so that they could be bought by more people. Although numerous other developments warrant mention,[3] I would like to concentrate on a single development that is of particular interest in the present context. The first common art market appeared in the 17th century in the Netherlands. Prior to this, all decisions as to what works of art were to be commissioned, what subjects were to be depicted, and what artists were to render the works were the exclusive domain of royalty and the church. Now, works by Jan Vermeer

Martini bianco, 2005
Wermut, 1 l
32,1 x 8,8 x 7,5 cm

Martini Bianco, 2005
Vermouth, 1 l
32.1 x 8.8 x 7.5 cm

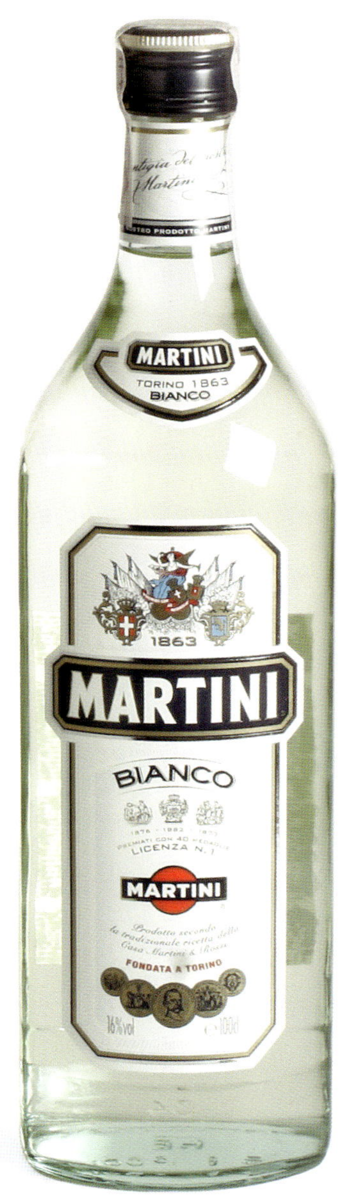

MARTINI
TORINO 1863
BIANCO
1863
MARTINI
BIANCO
LICENZA N.1
MARTINI
FONDATA A TORINO
16% vol

net war. Zuvor hatten Fürsten und Könige oder die Kirchen darüber entschieden, welche Kunst bei wem mit welchen Motiven in Auftrag gegeben werden sollte. Nun wurden auf Jahrmärkten zwischen Alltagsgegenständen, Trödel, Viehzeug, Kraut und Rüben, Jan Vermeers oder Pieter de Hoochs billig verkauft[4]. Mit ihren zahlreichen Bildern – bis zu 70 000 jährlich – orientierten sich die holländischen Künstler an einem gänzlich anderen Publikumsgeschmack, als dies in der bisherigen Kunstproduktion der Fall gewesen war, und popularisierten zugleich die Malerei. Die Entstehung des Konsums aus der Kunst in den Niederlanden verwandelte die Kunst zugleich in eine Ware.

Bis umgekehrt die Waren die Kunst eroberten, sollte es noch knapp 200 Jahre dauern. Diese historische Entwicklung ist

and Pieter de Hooch were sold cheaply at common market-places—among everyday utensils, livestock, cabbage and carrots.[4] Producing up to 70,000 paintings a year, the Dutch artists oriented themselves towards the tastes of their buyers and simultaneously popularized painting. This common trading of art in the Netherlands turned art into a commodity.

It would take another 200 years for the producers of consumer goods—in a reversal—to make use of art. This development can be seen in the history of advertising. Until the middle of the 19th century, advertising was limited to a small number of trading sectors, largely because the idea of leaving the market to its own devices was contrary to commercial and finance policy. With few exceptions, advertisements were not accepted in the reputable newspapers. It wasn't until the

Merz Spezial Dragees, 1999
60 Tabletten
Verpackung 9,8 x 5,2 x 3,8 cm

Merz Special Dragées, 1999
60 tablets
package size: 9.8 x 5.2 x 3.8 cm

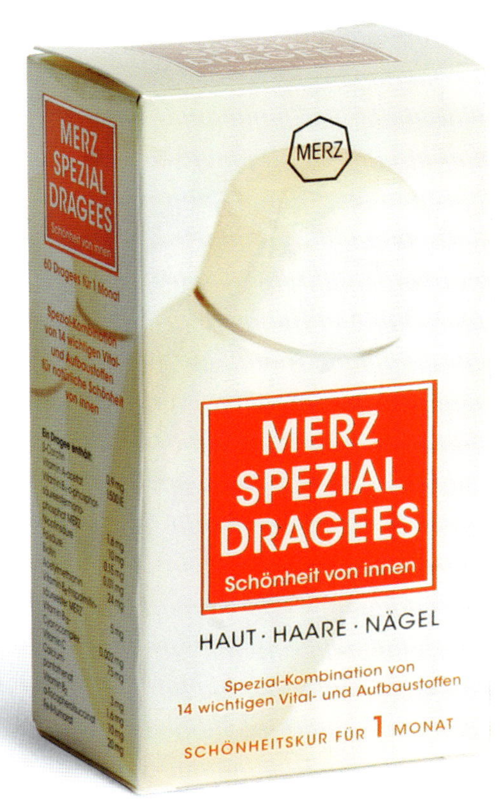
MERZ
MERZ SPEZIAL DRAGEES
Schönheit von innen
60 Dragees für 1 Monat
Spezial-Kombination von 14 wichtigen Vital- und Aufbaustoffen für natürliche Schönheit von innen
MERZ
SPEZIAL
DRAGEES
Schönheit von innen
HAUT · HAARE · NÄGEL
Spezial-Kombination von 14 wichtigen Vital- und Aufbaustoffen
SCHÖNHEITSKUR FÜR 1 MONAT

eingebunden in die Geschichte der Werbung. Bis Mitte des 19. Jahrhunderts beschränkten sich Werbeanzeigen auf einen kleinen Kreis von Gewerbezweigen, da es der merkantilistischen Wirtschafts- und Finanzpolitik widersprach, den Markt sich selbst zu überlassen. Gewerbliche Inserate wurden daher bis auf wenige Ausnahmen nicht in die »Intelligenzblätter« aufgenommen. Erst mit der Revolution von 1848/49 folgten zahlreiche Zeitungsneugründungen und der Aufschwung der Annoncenwerbung begann.[5]

Warum aber musste nun für Produkte geworben werden? Während bisher Verkäufer zumeist auch Produzenten waren, änderte sich dies im Laufe des 19. Jahrhunderts zunehmend. Zwischen Produkt, Produzent und Käufer traten Zwischenhändler. Damit Produkte, die nun immer seltener auf

revolution of 1848/49 and the subsequent founding of many new newspapers that newspaper advertising began in its own right.[5]

But why had it become necessary to advertise products? The situation in which the sellers of products were almost always the same as their producers changed dramatically in the course of the 19th century. Middlemen emerged to coordinate the sale of producers' goods to buyers. In order to ensure that products, which were now sold ever less frequently at weekly markets, could be transported in larger amounts over greater distances and could retain their quality for longer periods, they had to be packaged. Packaging introduced limitations to prospective buyers' ability to immediately inspect products using their senses of sight, smell and touch.

Michelangelo superscharf, 2005
Brotmesser
1 x 1,9 x 21,3 cm

Michelangelo Super Sharp, 2005
Bread knife
1 x 1.9 x 21.3 cm

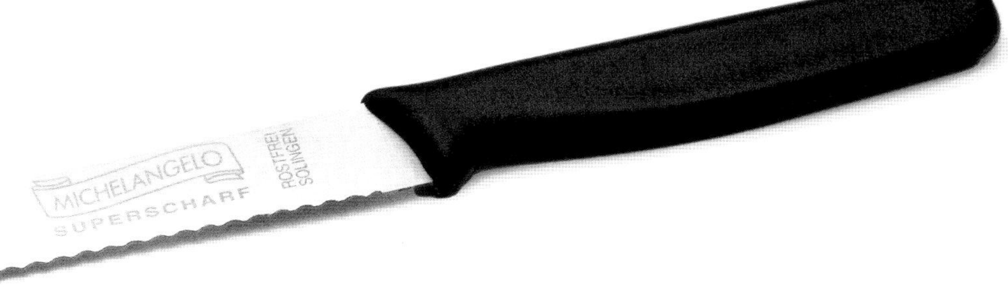
MICHELANGELO
SUPERSCHARF
ROSTFREI
SOLINGEN

Wochenmärkten verkauft wurden, über weitere Strecken in größeren Mengen transportiert werden konnten und damit sie länger haltbar waren, mussten sie verpackt werden. Nun war es nicht mehr möglich, Waren in Augenschein zu nehmen, an ihnen zu riechen, sie auf ihre Qualität hin zu testen. Die Werbung kann somit als Reaktion auf eine zunehmende Verunsicherung der Konsumenten gegenüber der Qualität von Waren gedeutet werden. Es musste enorm viel Vertrauen investiert werden, um z.B. Nahrungsmittel zu kaufen, die man weder sehen, noch riechen oder gar anfassen konnte. Auf den nun in sehr viel höherem Maße erforderten Vertrauensvorschuss antworteten die Unternehmen mit der Einführung von Marken. Die Marke hatte also eine doppelte Aufgabe: Sie sollte die ehemals persönliche Bindung zwi-

Advertising can thus be interpreted as a response on the part of producers and sellers to an increasing uncertainty among consumers with respect to the quality of products. Purchasing food that one could neither see, smell or touch required a certain degree of trust. Companies responded to the need to meet this higher degree of trust by introducing brands. These were required to play a dual role: they were to replace the former personal relationship between buyer and producer and they were to convey a sensory impression of goods that were hidden by packaging. A picture of what was no longer directly visible was to be created so as to help reduce the purchase risk felt by the consumer. While advertising was almost exclusively a matter of textual descriptions up as far as the 1890s, the use of recurring slogans and pictures became ever

Miro Femme
Eau de Parfum, 0,075 l
10,9 x 8,4 x 3,1 cm

Miro Femme
Eau de perfume, 0.075 l
10.9 x 8.4 x 3.1 cm

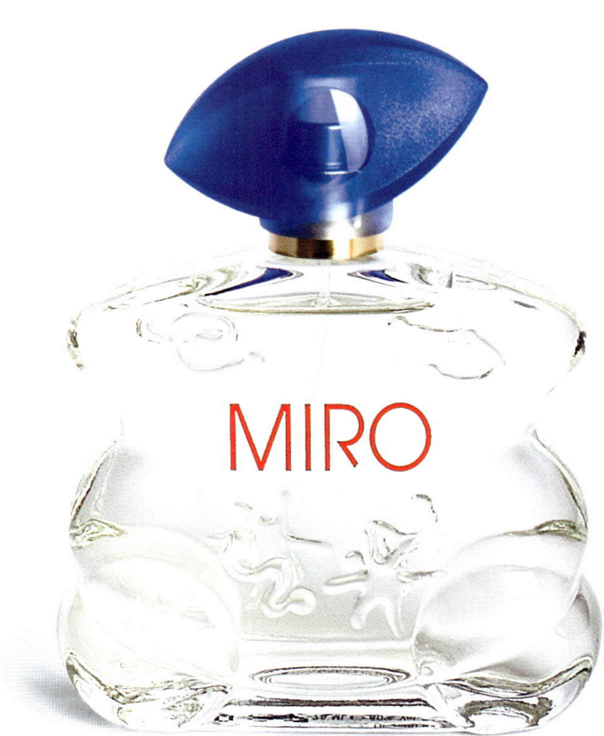
MIRO

schen Käufer und Produzent ersetzen und sie sollte nach Verschwinden eines sinnlichen Eindrucks der Ware alternative Sinneseindrücke vermitteln. So sollten eine Vorstellung des nicht mehr zu Sehenden erzeugt und das gefühlte Kaufrisiko des Konsumenten gesenkt werden. Während bis in die 1890er Jahre Werbung vor allem als textlastige Information verstanden wurde, wurde mit Aufkommen der ersten Marken der Einsatz von wiederkehrenden, möglichst knappen Schriftzügen immer wichtiger. Aber auch Bilder wurden nun in der Werbung immer bedeutsamer. Um 1900 begann die Werbung, von den Zeitungen ausgehend, die Großstädte der industrialisierten Metropolen zu erobern. Plakate, Leuchtwerbung, Fassadenmalerei, Litfaßsäulen – hier wurde die enge Verbindung des Produktes und seiner künstlerischen Vermarktung hergestellt.

more important following the introduction of brands. Around the year 1900, advertising—particularly in the major cities of the industrialized world—began to branch out beyond its newspaper base. Posters, neon signs, murals, and billboards became the media by which art was used to market products.

Art, commerce, and consumption now began to penetrate one another. It was self-evident in the young consumption-oriented society that consumption was more than a way of meeting needs, needs that may not even have been perceived prior to advertising. Consumption was always simultaneously charged with meaning, messages, and temptations. Advertising images were expected to conjure mental images. These images are places of convergence for commercial interests and a function traditionally fulfilled by art: the generation of

Monet-Goyon AL5, 1936
Motorrad 500 ccm
ca. 80 x 200 x 80 cm

Monet-Goyon AL5, 1936
Motorrad 500 ccm
c. 80 x 200 x 80 cm

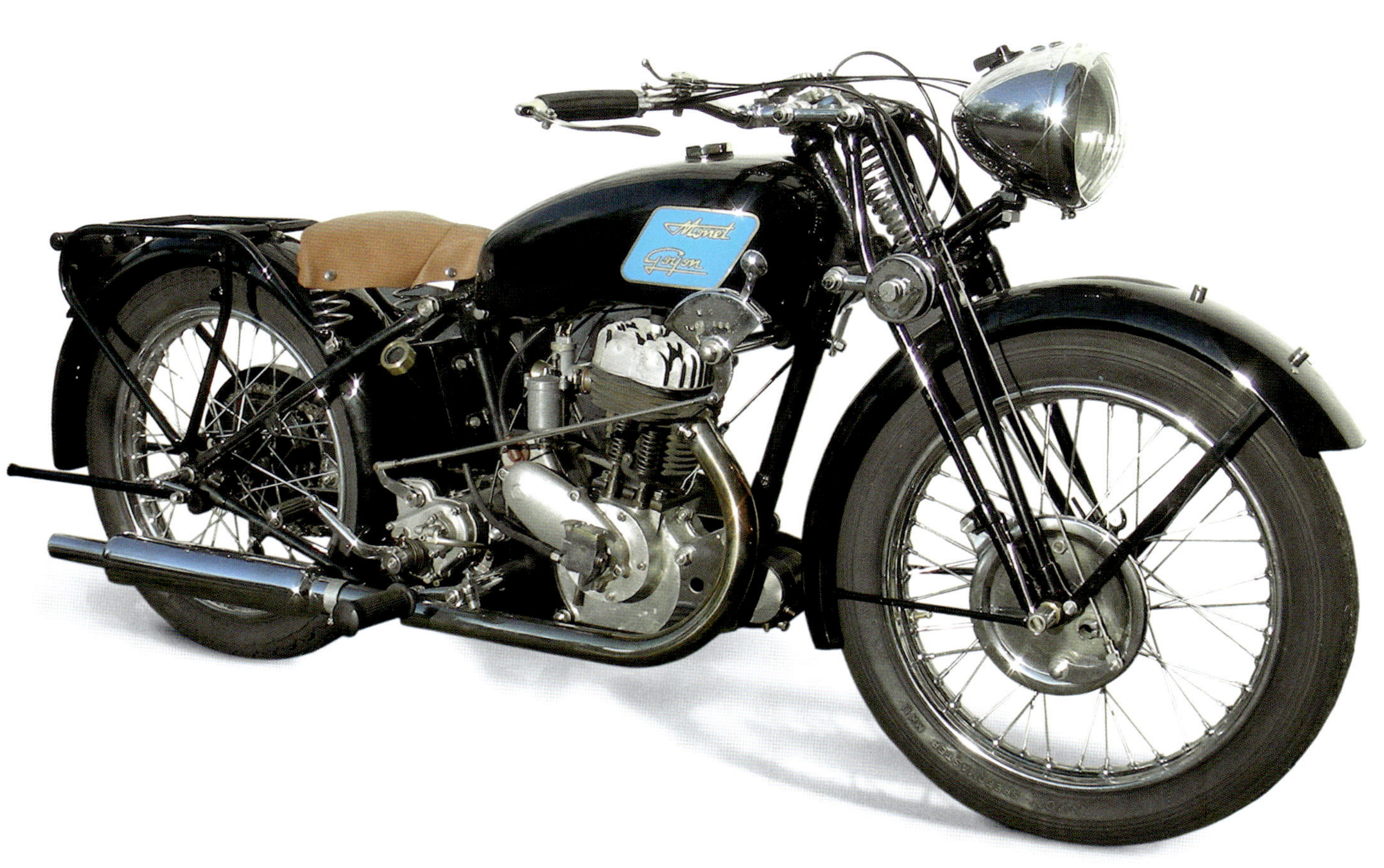
Monet
Goyon

Kunst, Kommerz und Konsum begannen nun, sich gegensei-
tig zu durchdringen. Konsum, das war der jungen Konsum-
gesellschaft schon selbstverständlich, diente nicht allein der
Erfüllung von Bedürfnissen, die eventuell vor der Werbung
niemand verspürt hatte. Konsum war stets zugleich aufgeladen mit Bedeutung, mit Botschaften, mit Verheißungen.
Werbebilder sollten innere Bilder hervorrufen, »Images«,
wie dies in der heutigen Marketingsprache genannt wird. Im
Image überkreuzt sich ein Interesse der Warenwelt mit der
Funktion, die Kunst traditioneller Weise erfüllte: die Gene-
rierung symbolischer Bedeutung. Wurde die Warenwelt zu
Beginn des 20. Jahrhunderts durch die künstlerische Werbung mit einer Aura aufgeladen, die der Kunst abhanden
kam? Walter Benjamin bezeichnete das Museum Mitte des

symbolic meaning. Did the artful means that were used in the
service of marketing products at the beginning of the 20th
century invest these products with the aura that had been
lost by traditional works of art? Walter Benjamin refers to the
museum of the mid 19th century as just one of many dream
venues that was not experienced differently by its visitors
than arcades, botanical gardens, wax-figure houses, casinos,
railway stations and department stores.[6]

When we examine the relationship between art, commerce,
and consumption from a historical perspective, we are naturally forced to include an account of the beholder or observer
referred to by Benjamin. In addition to the fundamental
changes that took place in the forms of interaction between
producers, consumers, dealers, and products in the course

Mueller's Dünne Spaghetti
Teigware, 227 g
5,5 x 2,6 x 25,8 cm

Mueller's Thin Spaghetti
Pasta, 227 g
5.5 x 2.6 x 25.8 cm

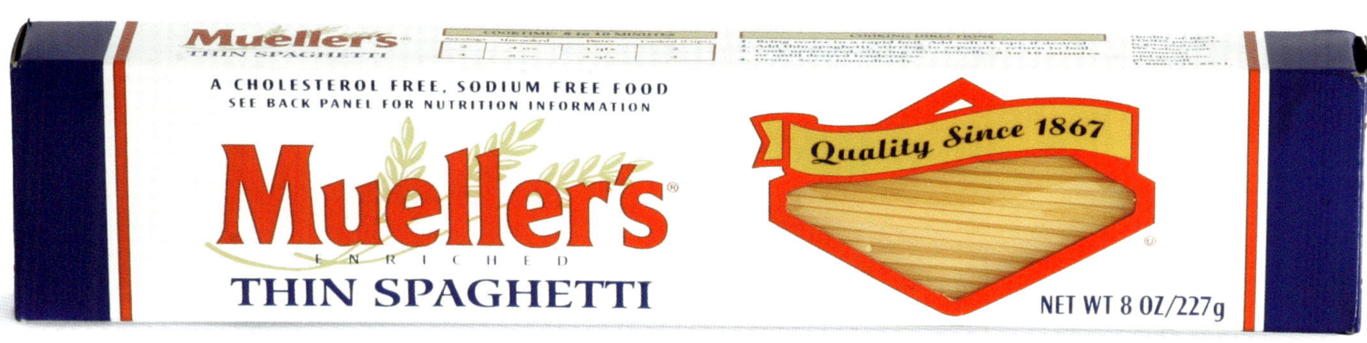

Mueller's
THIN SPAGHETTI
A CHOLESTEROL FREE, SODIUM FREE FOOD
SEE BACK PANEL FOR NUTRITION INFORMATION
Mueller's
ENRICHED
THIN SPAGHETTI
Quality Since 1867
NET WT 8 OZ/227g

19. Jahrhunderts als eines von vielen Traumhäusern, das von einem Betrachter nicht anders empfunden oder durchwandert werde als Passagen, Botanische Gärten, Wachsfigurenkabinette, Kasinos, Bahnhöfe und Kaufhäuser.[6]

Wenn wir die Beziehung von Kunst, Kommerz und Konsum untersuchen und sie historisch beleuchten, müssen wir den hier von Benjamin zitierten Betrachter mit einbeziehen. Im Laufe des 19. Jahrhunderts hat sich nicht nur die Interaktionsform zwischen Produzent, Konsument, Händler und Ware grundlegend verändert. Es haben sich auch die »Techniken des Betrachters« verändert.[7] Ein Betrachter, sei es der Betrachter eines Kunstwerkes, einer Fotografie oder eines Werbeplakats, ist jemand, der in ein System von Konventionen, von Regeln, von Zuschreibung eingebettet ist. Er sieht

of the 19th century, the "techniques" of the beholder or observer also changed.[7] A beholder, whether the beholder of a painting, photograph or advertising poster, is someone who is embedded in a system of conventions, rules, and attributes. Observers observe within a framework that specifies what they can see. Vision is also a historical construct. In the course of the 19th century, vision was released from its fixed, internal and external points of reference. What Jonathan Crary referred to as the "automation of vision"[8] began. With a variety of means, the activity of the eye had now been newly codified and controlled.

Modern studies of consumer behavior have shown that the relationship between advertising and consumption is not monocausal.[9] It is not only advertising that attempts to charge

Newman's Own, 2000
Venezianische Spaghettisauce mit Pilzen, 737 g
Höhe 16,7 cm, ⌀ 8,9 cm

Newman's Own, 2000
Venetian Spaghetti Sauce with Mushrooms, 737 g
height: 16.7 cm, ⌀ 8.9 cm

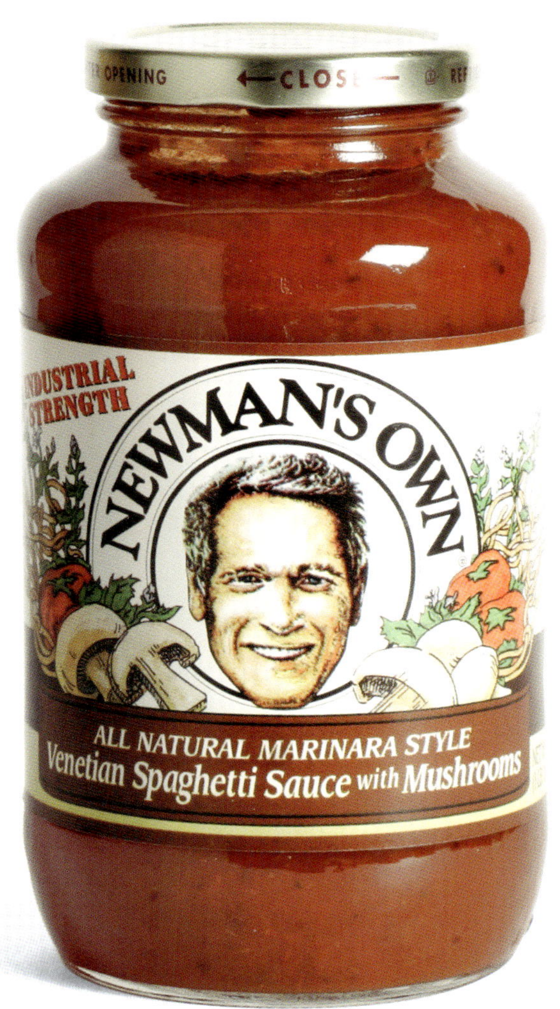
CLOSE
INDUSTRIAL
STRENGTH
NEWMAN'S OWN
ALL NATURAL MARINARA STYLE
Venetian Spaghetti Sauce with Mushrooms

innerhalb eines Rahmens, der ihm vorgibt, was er sehen kann. Das Sehen ist ebenfalls eine historische Konstruktion. Im Laufe des 19. Jahrhunderts wird das Sehen von seinen festen Bezugspunkten von Innen/Außen losgelöst. Es beginnt, was Jonathan Crary die »Autonomisierung des Sehens«[8] genannt hat. Das Sehen macht sich selbstständig. Mit einer Vielfalt an Mitteln wurde die Aktivität der Augen nun neu codiert und neu gelenkt.

Aus der modernen Konsumforschung wissen wir längst, dass sich Werbung und Konsum nicht monokausal aufeinander beziehen lassen.[9] Nicht nur die Werbung versucht den Konsum mit Bedeutung aufzuladen, auch Konsumenten lassen sich als Sinnproduzenten verstehen, je nachdem wie und mit welchem Ziel sie sich Konsumgüter aneignen.

consumption with meaning. Consumers may also be regarded as creators of meaning, depending on how and with what aim they acquire consumer goods.

By way of summary, we can connect the three historical stages outlined above. First, there was the emergence of art as an object of commerce in the 17th century. Then, around 1900, advertisers exploited art in an attempt to ennoble consumption. Finally, a century we find observers who may or may not be in a position to (or wish to) draw a connection between consumer goods and artists. The freedom of the observer is naturally limited, with vision itself being subject to the subtle mechanisms of control present throughout the modern age.

Citroën C4 Picasso, 2007

Kombilimousine

161-166,5 x 446,8 x 183,1 cm

Citroën C4 Picasso, 2007

Minivan

161-166.5 x 446.8 x 183.1 cm

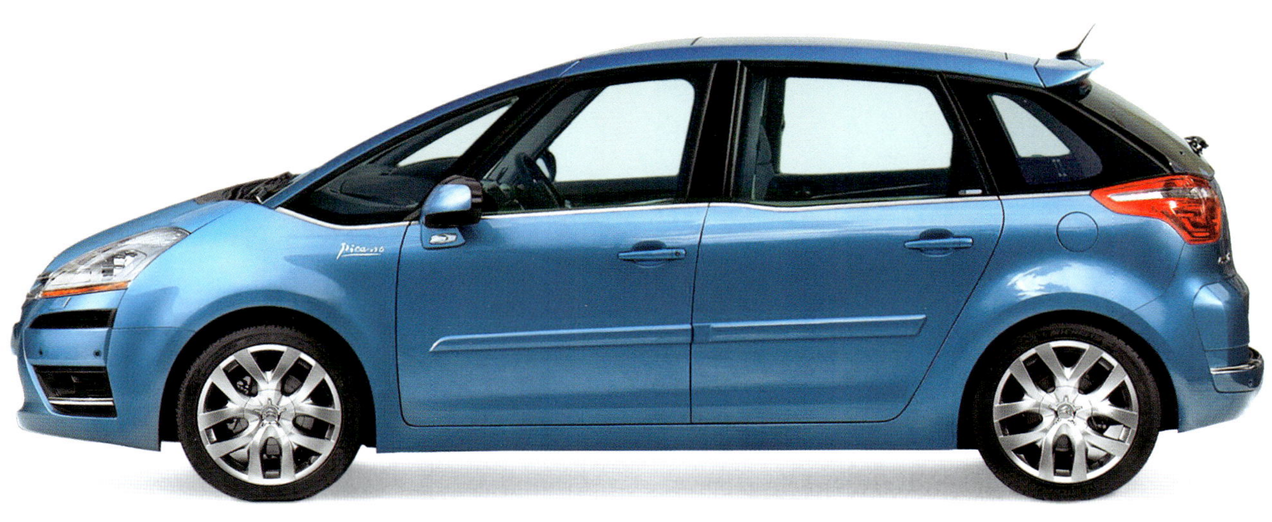

Wir können die drei genannten, historischen Etappen aufeinander beziehen. Am Anfang meiner Überlegungen stand die Entwicklung des Konsums aus der Kunst im 17. Jahrhundert. Die Kunst wurde zur Ware. Um 1900 eroberte die Werbung die Kunst und versuchte, den Konsum mit Kunst zu adeln. Ein weiteres Jahrhundert später sind wir auf den Betrachter verwiesen, der Bezüge zwischen Waren und Künstlern herzustellen (ver-)mag oder nicht. Seine Freiheit ist freilich eng begrenzt und den subtilen Lenkungen und Codierungen unseres Blicks unterworfen, wie sie die Moderne durchziehen.

Wenn es der Ausstellung »ArtBrands« gelingt, den Blick der Konsumenten auf »ihre« Waren so zu verändern, dass sie sich des Blicks auf und der Aneignung von Konsumgütern bewusst werden, dann hat sie bereits in die Sehgewohnheiten eingegriffen. Die Frage nach der Aura der Kunst und der Werbung lässt sich nicht oder leicht beantworten: Sie liegt im Auge des Betrachters/Konsumenten. ■

If the exhibition "ArtBrands" changes the view consumers take of "their" products so that they become aware of this view and the acquisition of such products, then it will have succeeded in intervening in their visual habits. The question about the aura of art and advertising is difficult to answer: it is ultimately in the eye of the beholder/consumer. ■

Raffaello, 2007
Kokos-Mandel-Konfekt, 230 g
19 x 14 x 9,5 cm

Raffaello, 2007
Coconut almond confectionery, 230 g
19 x 14 x 9.5 cm

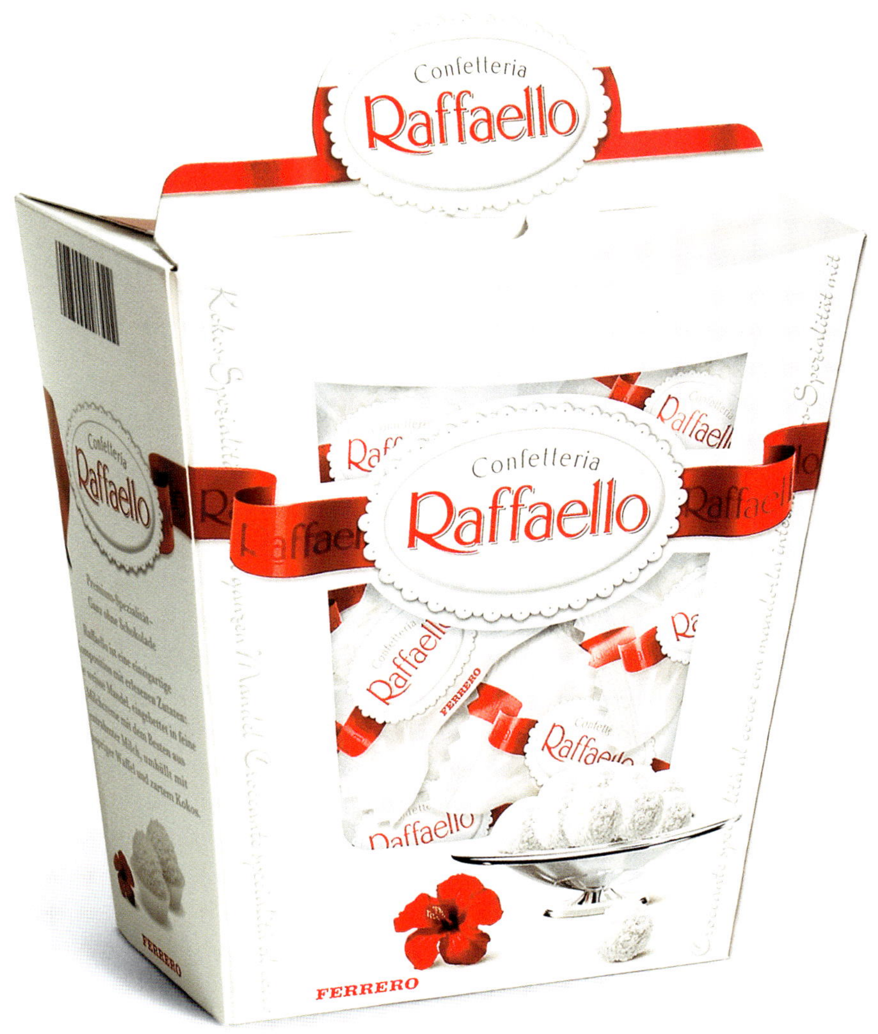

Confetteria
Raffaello
Confetteria
Raffaello
FERRERO

1 Walter Benjamin, Das Kunstwerk im Zeitalter seiner technischen Reproduzierbarkeit (1936), Frankfurt am Main 1963.

2 Dominik Schrage, Auf der Schwelle zur Konsumsoziologie. Aspekte der Konsumkritik in den fünfziger Jahren – ein Prolog, in: Kai-Uwe Hellmann, Dominik Schrage (2004), S. 13–32, hier: S. 13.

3 Einen gelungenen Überblick gibt Heinz-Gerhard Haupt, Konsum und Handel. Europa im 19. und 20. Jahrhundert, Göttingen 2003.

4 Joachim Fischer, Warenwerbung und Warentest oder Poetismus und Rationalismus. Komplementäre Sozialmechanismen in der bürgerlichen Massenkultur, in: Kai-Hellmann, Dominik Schrage (Hg.), Konsum der Werbung, S. 49–62, hier: S. 53.

5 Vgl. zur Entwicklung der Werbung: Dirk Reinhard, Von der Reklame zum Marketing. Geschichte der Wirtschaftswerbung in Deutschland, Berlin 1993.

6 Walter Benjamin, Passagenwerk, in: Gesammelte Schriften, Bd. V 1, S. 510–523, Frankfurt am Main 1982.

7 Jonathan Crary, Techniken des Betrachters. Sehen und Moderne im 19. Jahrhundert, Dresden, Basel 1996.

8 Ebd., S. 30.

9 Kai-Uwe Hellmann, Dominik Schrage (Hg.), Konsum der Werbung. Zur Produktion und Rezeption von Sinn in der kommerziellen Kultur, Wiesbaden 2004, S. 8

1 Walter Benjamin, "The Work of Art in the Age of Mechanical Reproduction (1936)," Frankfurt, 1963.

2 Dominik Schrage, "Auf der Schwelle zur Konsumsoziologie. Aspekte der Konsumkritik in den fünfziger Jahren—ein Prolog" in: Kai-Uwe Hellmann, Dominik Schrage (2004), pp. 13–32, here: p. 13.

3 Heinz-Gerhard Haupt offers a helpful overview in "Konsum und Handel. Europa im 19. und 20. Jahrhundert," Göttingen 2003.

4 Joachim Fischer, "Warenwerbung und Warentest oder Poetismus und Rationalismus. Komplementäre Sozialmechanismen in der bürgerlichen Massenkultur" in: Kai-Hellmann, Dominik Schrage, "Konsum der Werbung," pp. 49–62, here: p. 53.

5 For a discussion of the development of advertising, see: Dirk Reinhard, "Von der Reklame zum Marketing. Geschichte der Wirtschaftswerbung in Deutschland," Berlin 1993.

6 Walter Benjamin, "Passagenwerk" in: Gesammelte Schriften, Bd. V 1, pp. 510–523, Frankfurt 1982.

7 Jonathan Crary, Techniques of the Observer: On Vision and Modernity in the 19th Century, Dresden, Basel 1996.

8 Ibid. p. 30.

9 Kai-Uwe Hellmann, Dominik Schrage, "Konsum der Werbung. Zur Produktion und Rezeption von Sinn in der kommerziellen Kultur," Wiesbaden 2004, p. 8.

Rauch SU602, 2007
Winterdienststreuer
142 x 132 x 220 cm

Rauch SU602, 2007
Gritter
142 x 132 x 220 cm

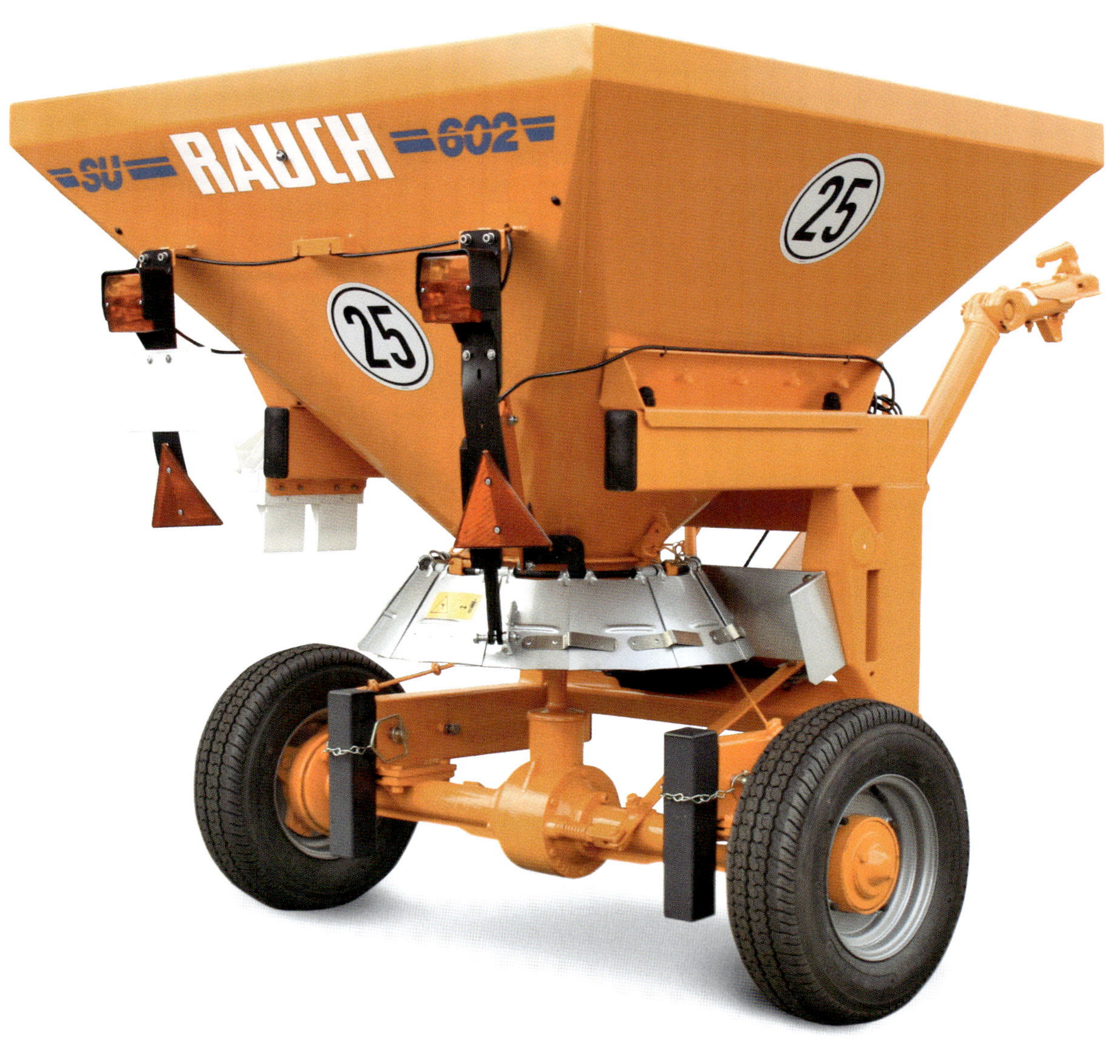

SU RAUCH 602
25
25

Manfred Gotta

Ein Rembrandt für $9.95 | A Rembrandt for $9.95

Ein Rembrandt für $9.95 – solch ein Angebot könnte in der Öffentlichkeit, bei Museen und Kunstsammlern durchaus einen Schock auslösen. Es fallen einem unglaublich wertvolle Gemälde oder berühmte Auktionshäuser ein, wo man einen Rembrandt eventuell für Millionenbeträge ersteigern kann – wenn überhaupt. Aber Rembrandt ist nicht gleich Rembrandt. In Amerika putzen sich viele Menschen die Zähne mit Rembrandt, denn dort wird unter diesem Namen eine Zahncreme verkauft, die knapp unter 10 Dollar kostet. Im Vergleich mit anderen Zahncremes ist die Zahncreme Rembrandt verdammt teuer – der Name verpflichtet eben.

A Rembrandt for $9.95 — such an offer could be expected to trigger chaos of epic proportions, as prospective buyers from around the world rushed to get to the point of sale on time. What comes to mind are paintings of unbelievable value, usually sold at the world's premier auction houses for millions of dollars. But Rembrandt is not always the same as Rembrandt. In America, for instance, a lot of people brush their teeth with Rembrandt because Rembrandt in America is also a brand of toothpaste, costing just under 10 dollars for a 3-ounce tube. Now, compared to other kinds of toothpaste, Rembrandt is pretty darned expensive, but maybe the higher price is a way of meeting an obligation that comes with the name.

Rembrandt, 1997
Zahnpasta, 85 g
6,5 x 17,6 x 2,9 cm

Rembrandt, 1997
Toothpaste, 85 g
6.5 x 17.6 x 2.9 cm

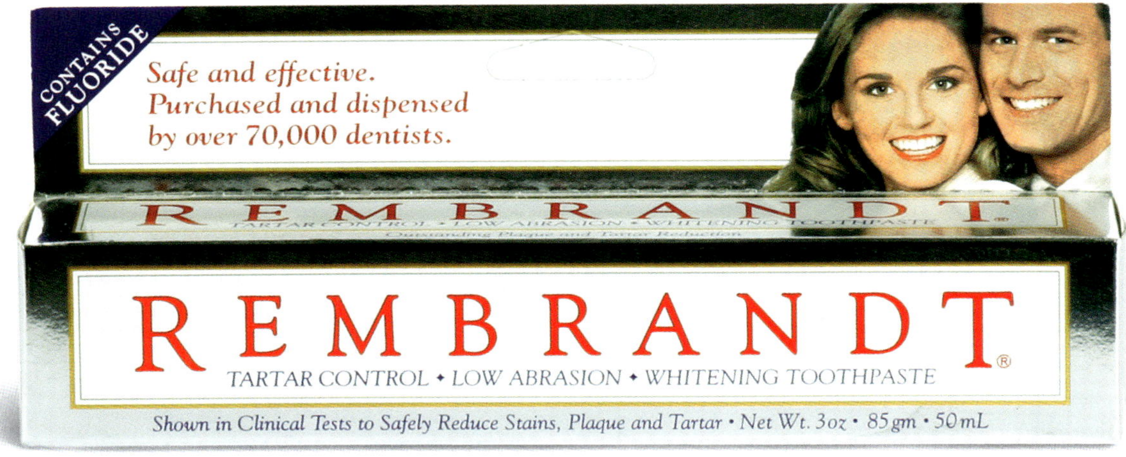
CONTAINS FLUORIDE
Safe and effective.
Purchased and dispensed
by over 70,000 dentists.
REMBRANDT
TARTAR CONTROL • LOW ABRASION • WHITENING TOOTHPASTE
Outstanding Plaque and Tartar Reduction
REMBRANDT
TARTAR CONTROL • LOW ABRASION • WHITENING TOOTHPASTE
Shown in Clinical Tests to Safely Reduce Stains, Plaque and Tartar • Net Wt. 3oz • 85 gm • 50 mL

Es liegt am Namen, an der wichtigsten Identifikationsmöglich-
keit, die es gibt. Man kennt ja den Spruch: »Wo Nutella drauf
steht, muss Nutella drin sein« – aber man sieht, dass man sich
offensichtlich nicht immer darauf verlassen kann.

Die ganze Welt kennt Rembrandt als einen der großen Maler
der Kunstgeschichte, und so hat man ihn im Hirn abgespei-
chert. Auf entsprechende Fragen nach diesem Namen kommen also heute schon vorher bekannte Antworten. Dass es
tatsächlich auch eine Zahncreme gibt, deren Produktname
Rembrandt heißt, käme uns gar nicht erst in den Sinn.

Das ist bei allen großen Namen so, und deshalb wären wir
ebenso irritiert, wenn wir von Chiquita-Pflaumen erzählt bekä-
men oder von Tabasco-Zucker.

What is at issue here is the name — the most important means
of identification available. In Germany, many are familiar with a
Nutella advertising slogan that assures its customers that anything labeled Nutella will also contain Nutella. But as we have
seen, we may not always be able to rely on such assurances.

Rembrandt is known around the world as one of the greatest
painters in the history of art. This is the way we have stored
the name in our brains. Our answers to questions about
the name Rembrandt are accordingly predictable. It usually
wouldn't even occur to us that there is also a brand of toothpaste that goes by the name of Rembrandt.

The same essentially applies to all great names. We would be
similarly perplexed if we were told of Chiquita plums or Tabasco

Richter Feuer-Röllchen, 2001
Heringsfilets, 120 g
Höhe 4,3 cm, ⌀ 10,1 cm

Richter Fire Rolls, 2001
Herring fillets, 120 g
height: 4.3 cm, ⌀ 10.1 cm

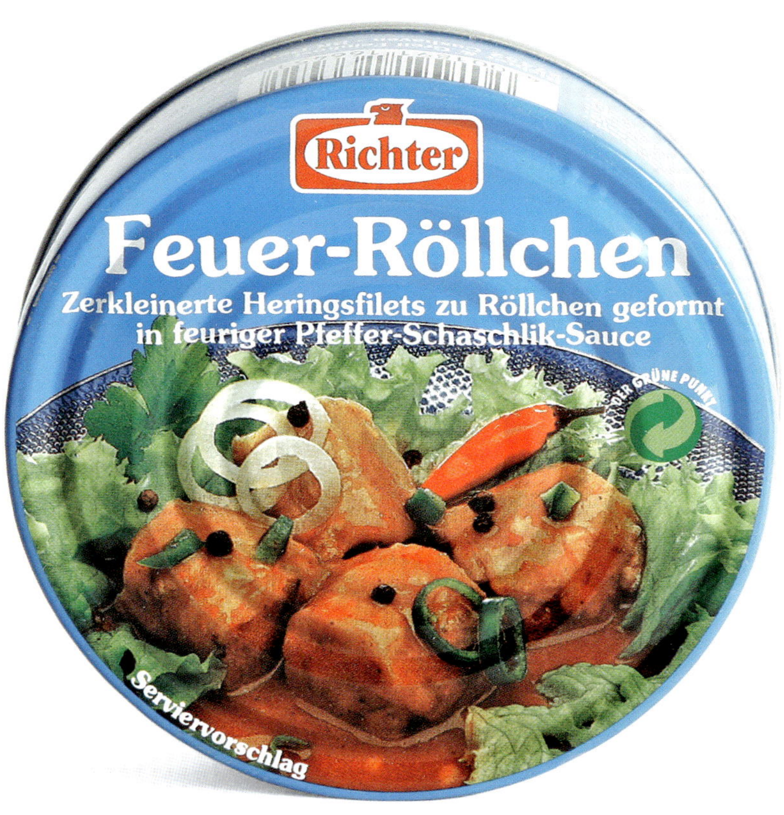

Richter
Feuer-Röllchen
Zerkleinerte Heringsfilets zu Röllchen geformt
in feuriger Pfeffer-Schaschlik-Sauce
Serviervorschlag

Unsere Reaktion und auch die im Ausland wäre, Chiquita sind doch Bananen und Tabasco ist – vom mexikanischen Bundesstaat einmal abgesehen – eine scharfe Soße. Wir fragen uns auch nicht, was heißt eigentlich Chiquita oder Tabasco, und eigentlich interessiert es uns auch nicht, denn wir haben gelernt, was diese Namen bedeuten.

Dass große Namen eine so einzigartige und klare Bedeutung haben, ist auf der einen Seite das größte Kapital für ihre Besitzer, auf der anderen Seite jedoch auch eine Einschränkung.

Große Namen haben nahezu immer eine klare und eindeutige Botschaft, die manchmal bis hin zum Klischee oder Vorurteil führt. BMW ist Sportlichkeit, Marlboro Abenteuer oder Volvo Sicherheit – und bei Volvo hört man immer noch, dass

sugar. Our reaction, and that of others in many other countries, would be to point out that Chiquita is a brand of bananas and Tabasco—except for being the name of a Mexican state—is a kind of hot sauce. We also don't ask ourselves what Chiquita and Tabasco actually mean. The issue doesn't even interest us because we have already learned what these names mean.

Although the exceptionally clear and unique meaning of great names constitutes the most important asset for their owners, it also represents a limitation.

Great names almost always have a clear and unique message that can sometimes degenerate into a cliché or bias. BMW is inevitably associated with sportiness, Marlboro with adventure and Volvo with safety. We still often hear that Volvos

Rietveld, 2000
T-Shirt (Rückseite)
Größe M

Rietveld, 2000
T-shirt (back)
size M

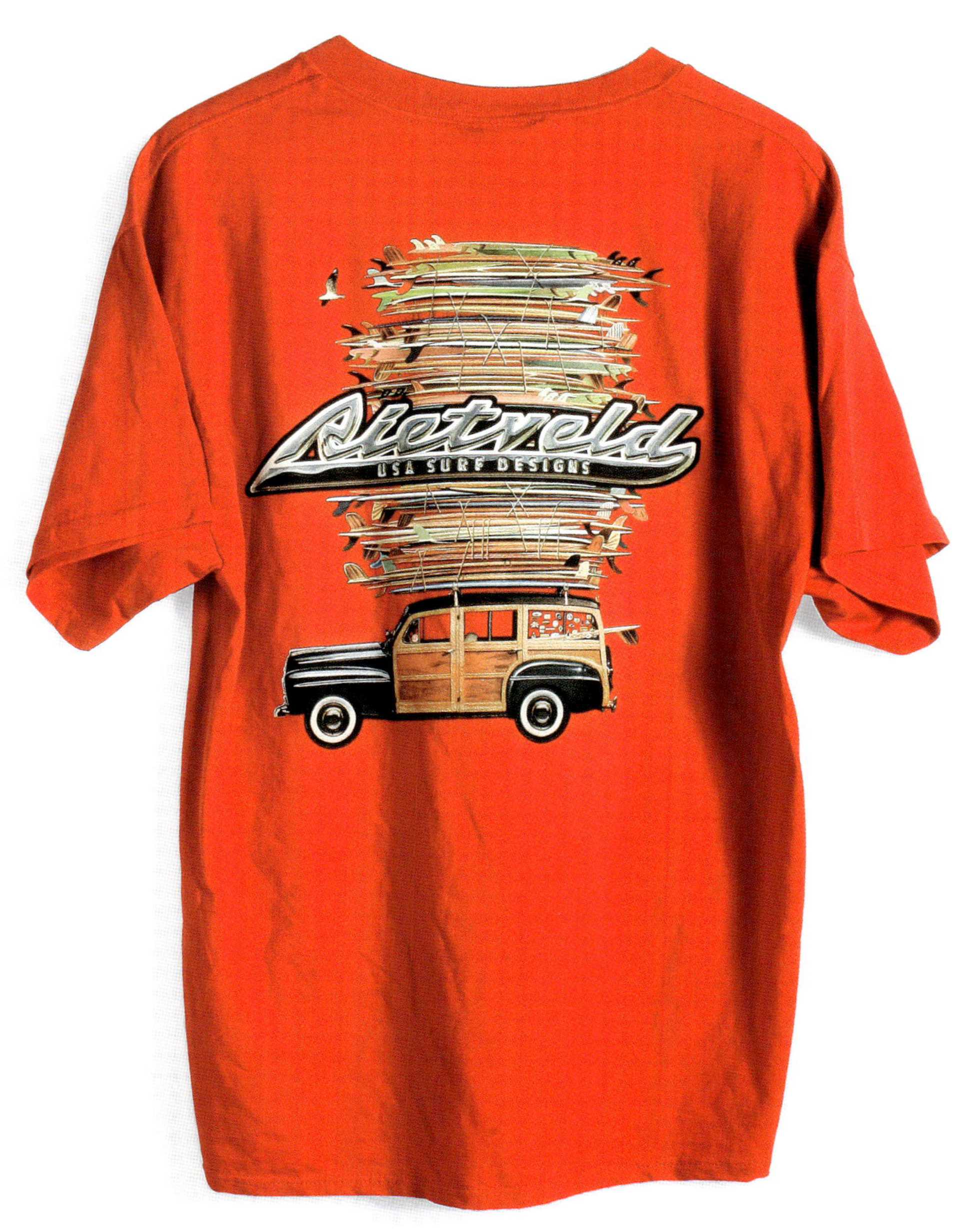
Rietveld
USA SURF DESIGNS

das Blech dicker sei als bei anderen Autos, was natürlich nie stimmte, aber in den Köpfen der Menschen verankert ist. Man kann Mercedes fahren, rauchen oder an den Füßen tragen. Aber das erste, woran man denkt, ist das Auto.

Es stellt sich die Frage, warum wir bestimmte Namen so genau kennen und welchen Sinn es macht, wenn man als Hersteller genau so heißt oder ein Produkt mit einem solchen Namen benennen will – sieht man einmal von der rechtlichen Situation ab, auf die noch eingegangen wird.

Während die meisten sich unter Michelangelo noch Küchenutensilien vorstellen können, sofern sie über ein schönes Design verfügen, wird sich wohl bei Trommelhäckslern von Vermeer doch die Frage stellen, ob ein anderer Name hierfür nicht geeigneter wäre. Der Grund ist einfach. Bei Michelange-

are made with thicker metal than other cars, a claim that was naturally never true, however firmly anchored it was and remains in the heads of people. Although products named Mercedes can be driven, smoked or worn on our feet, what we think of first when we hear the name is the car.

The question arises as to why we know certain names so well, and what is to be gained when one, as a manufacturer, shares a famous name or would like to use such a name for a certain product—disregarding for the moment the legal situation, which I will come to.

While most people will find Michelangelo kitchenware plausible, as long as it has an appealing design, the use of the name Vermeer in connection with a gasoline-powered brush chipper might be a disadvantage. The reason is simple. In the

Schick Slim Twin ST, 1998
Fünf Nassrasierer
Verpackung 12,4 x 12,6 x 2 cm

Schick Slim Twin ST, 1998
Five razors
package size: 12.4 x 12.6 x 2 cm

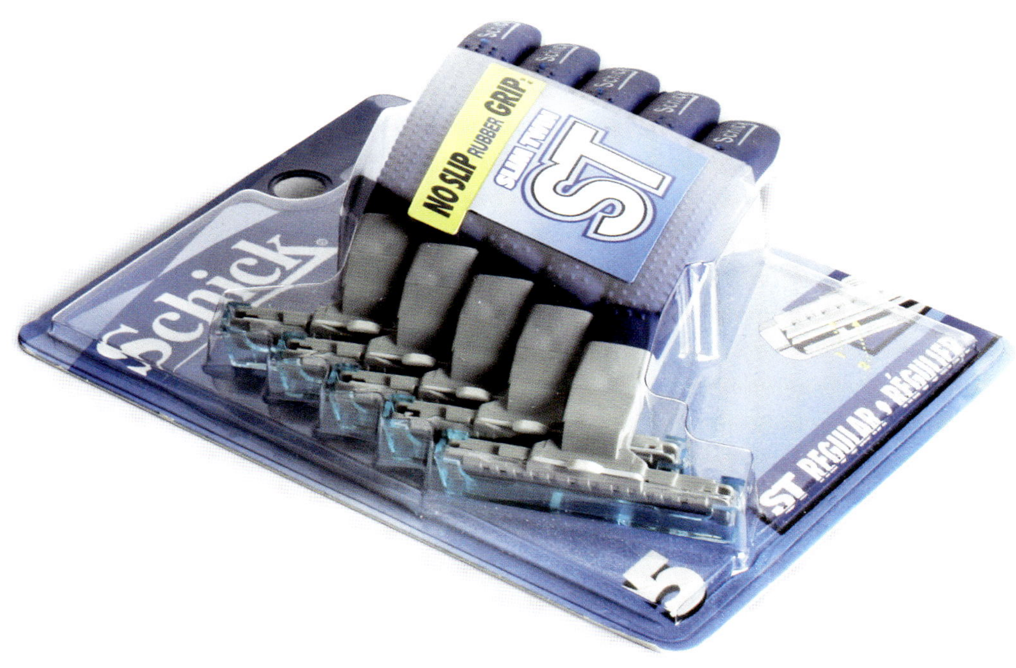
Schick
NO SLIP RUBBER GRIP
SLIM TWIN ST
5
ST REGULAR • RÉGULIER
5

lo und Küchenutensilien vermuten wir ein besonderes Design – sonst würden sie nicht so heißen. Bei Vermeer könnte man durchaus auch an eine Tapetenkollektion denken, an einen Trommelhäcksler aber mit Sicherheit sehr viel weniger.

Bekannte Namen haben über ihre konkrete Bedeutung hinaus noch eine andere Eigenart, sie strahlen Kompetenz aus. Michelangelo, Goya oder Vermeer »bedeuten« Kreativität, was den Schluss zulässt, dass man unter diesen Namen auch »schöne«, »kreative« und »hochwertige« Produkte teurer verkaufen kann. Bei Goya Dosenwürstchen fragt man sich automatisch, was Würstchen mit Goya oder Kunst zu tun haben, und damit wird das Produkt der Lächerlichkeit preisgegeben, die Absicht durchschaut.

case of Michelangelo and kitchenware, we rightly anticipate a special design. In the case of Vermeer, we might imagine a wallpaper collection, but not a brush chipper.

In addition to their concrete meaning, famous names also convey a sense of competence. Michelangelo, Goya, and Vermeer "mean" creativity. This makes it safer to conclude that one could also use these names to sell "beautiful," "creative," and "high-quality" products at a good price. In the case of Goya sausage in a jar, we are more inclined to ask ourselves what sausage could possibly have to do with Goya or art. With its intention transparent, the product is exposed to ridicule.

Sierra bali, 2005
Strandmuschel
offen 120 x 250 x 110 cm / verpackt ca. 62 cm, ⌀ 13 cm

Sierra bali, 2005
Beach tent
open: 120 x 250 x 110 cm / packed: 62 cm, ⌀ 13 cm

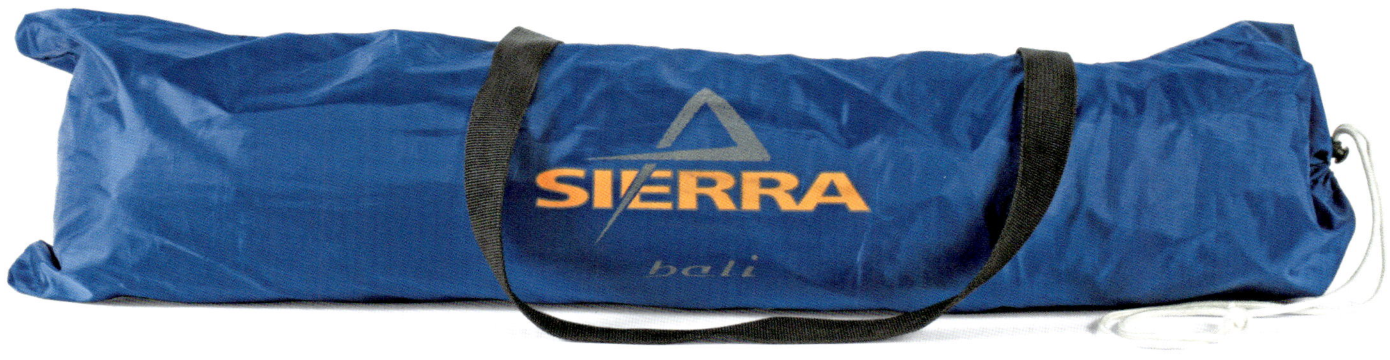

Der Name Odol Mundwasser bedeutet Kompetenz für den Mundbereich. Dass man dann auch die Zahncreme für ein glaubwürdiges und zum Namen passendes Produkt hält, ist nachvollziehbar. Eine Odol Bohrmaschine wäre sicherlich eine auffallende Bezeichnung – allerdings mit einer vorhersehbaren Reaktion durch den Betrachter. So wird es sicher auch bei der Ausstellung »ArtBrands« eine Vielzahl von Reaktionen geben, die vom Staunen bis hin zum Lachen geht.

Wie kommt es, dass große Namen in unterschiedlichsten Ländern und unterschiedlichsten Sprachen eine einheitliche Bedeutung haben können? Hier beginnt die Faszination von Namen und deren Wirkung. Ein Beispiel soll das verdeutlichen: Bevor ein Kind auf die Welt kommt, sucht man nach dem passenden Namen. Das Kind muss eine Identität haben. Auf

The name Odol Mouthwash signifies competence in the area of oral hygiene. It therefore comes as no surprise that people also regard the name Odol as suitable for toothpaste. While the name Odol for a drill would surely stand out, the reactions on the part of consumers would be rather predictable. The present exhibition called "ArtBrands" can be expected to elicit a wide variety of reactions, ranging from astonishment to amusement and mirth.

How is it that great names have a uniform meaning in various countries and various languages? This is where the fascination for names and their impact begins. For instance, we look for a fitting name before a child is born. The child must have an identity. We usually want to have a name that is appealing without giving the child an overly exotic label and therefore

Sisley, 2007
Damenschuhe Größe 37
6,9 x 24,8 x 8,4 cm

Sisley, 2007
Women's shoes, size 6
6.9 x 24.8 x 8.4 cm

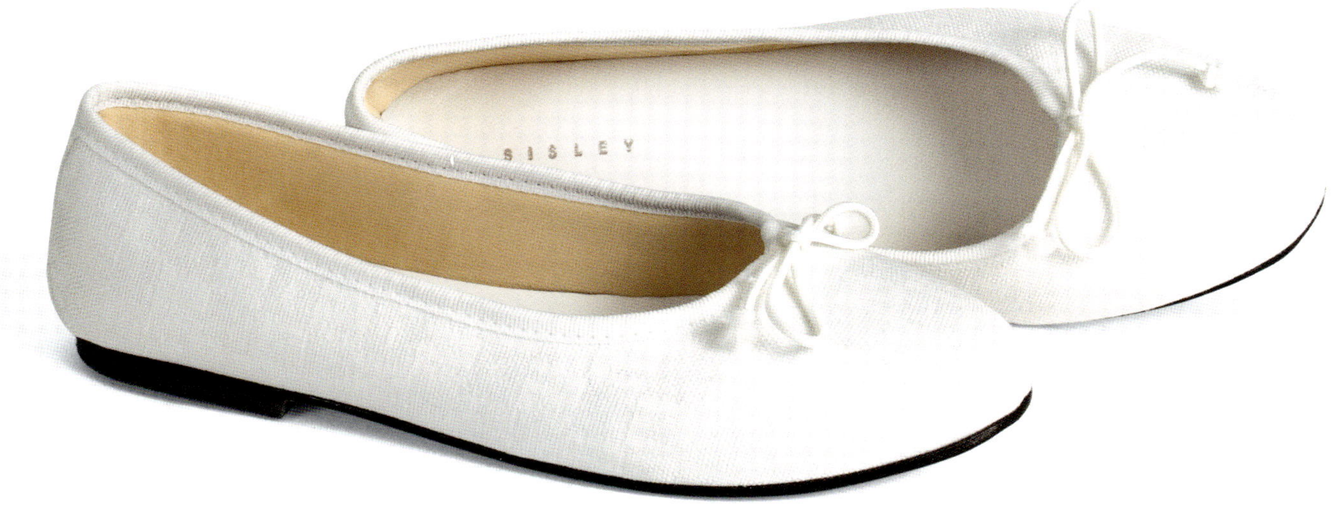

der anderen Seite will man mehrheitlich einen Namen, der gefällt, zugleich aber auch so ist, dass er das Kind nicht als exotische Erscheinung kennzeichnet und ihm dann schadet. Das »Produkt« ist ja noch nicht sichtbar, man kennt seine Eigenschaften noch nicht, und deshalb ist das so schwer.

Das Schlimmste in dieser Situation wäre, andere Personen zu fragen. Der Name Willy für den erwarteten Sohn kann dann die unterschiedlichsten Reaktionen hervorrufen. Einer sagt, das ist doch ein pfiffiger Name, der andere sagt, da kenne ich einen, der hat viel getrunken und hatte immer wieder Weiber. Rein gesprochene und existierende Namen werden dann rational und nach persönlicher »Erfahrung« bewertet, und die kann so oder so sein.

doing it a disservice. But we can't see the "product" yet. We don't know its distinctive qualities. These unknowns make it so difficult.

The worst thing to do in this situation is to ask other people — for instance, when we say, "What do you think of the name Willy"? The question is likely to elicit very different reactions. One might say that it is a smart and assertive-sounding name while another might relate a story about another Willy he knows who inherited a lot of money, never worked a day in his life, and is altogether obnoxious. Spoken and existing names are then evaluated rationally and according to one's personal experience.

Stella, 2005
Hartweizengrieß, 500 g
21,9 x 10,5 x 3,5 cm

Stella, 2005
Durum wheat semolina, 500 g
21.9 x 10.5 x 3.5 cm

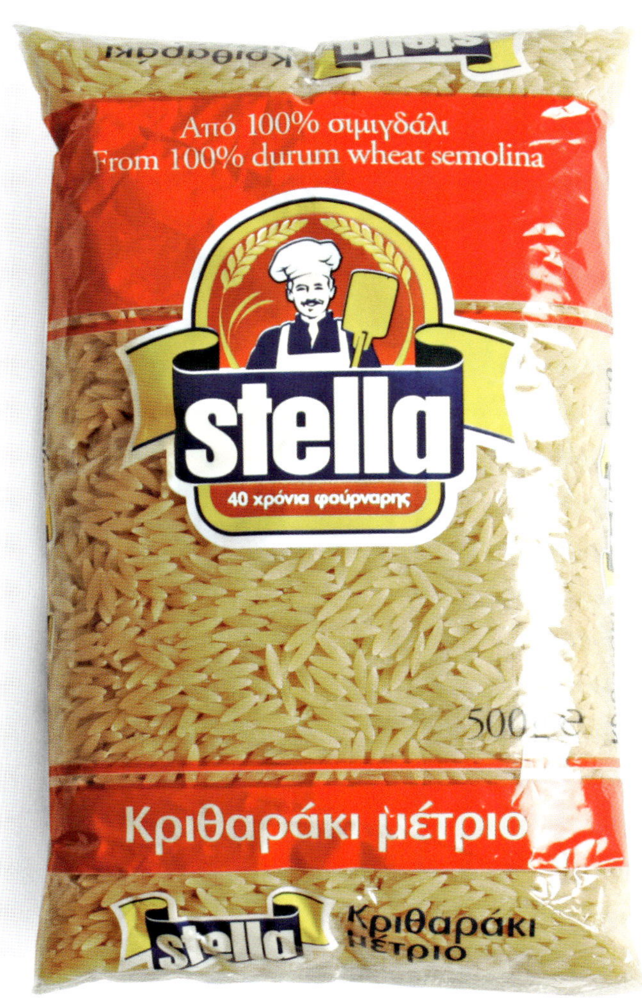

Από 100% σιμιγδάλι
From 100% durum wheat semolina
stella
40 χρόνια φούρναρης
500 g
Κριθαράκι μέτριο
stella
Κριθαράκι μέτριο

Im Falle eines konkreten neuen Produktes ist das schon einfacher, man kann es eben sehen und kennt die Eigenschaften. Man stelle sich folgende Situation vor: Ich nenne den Namen TIONY vor einer Gruppe von Menschen aus unterschiedlichsten Ländern. Jeder wird sich automatisch fragen, was das ist. Das Hirn kommt in Bewegung, es findet aber kein »Fach« mit dem Namen TIONY. Was machen die Menschen in so einer Situation? Sie fragen »Was ist das?« Und jeder stellt in seiner Sprache die Frage »Was ist TIONY?« Jetzt kann ich das Produkt vorstellen und sagen »TIONY ist ein völlig neuer zweifarbiger Diamant«. Und dieser Satz »ist ein neuer zweifarbiger Diamant« ist in jede Sprache der Welt übersetzbar. In diesem Moment lernen also alle Teilnehmer, was TIONY bedeutet. Ist der Name einzigartig und kommt dann intensive Kommunika-

It is easier in the case of a specific new product. We have the advantage of being able to see it and its properties. Imagine the following situation: I refer to a product called TIONY in front of a group of people from various countries. Those in the group will automatically ask themselves what the name means. Their brain cells fire, but they can't find a compartment for the name TIONY. What do people typically do in such situations? They ask, "What is that?" Then they all ask in their own language, "What is TIONY?" Now I can present the product and say, "TIONY is a completely new two-colored diamond," a statement that can be translated into any language in the world. At this very moment, all of the participants have learned what TIONY means. If the name is unique and if it continues to be presented using effective communication,

Tanguy Sablés pur beurre aux deux chocolats, 2006
Butter-Mürbekeks mit zwei Schokoladensorten, 150 g
9,8 x 27,5 x 3,7 cm

Tanguy Sablés pur beurre aux deux chocolats, 2006
Shortbread with two sorts of chocolate, 150 g
9.8 x 27.5 x 3.7 cm

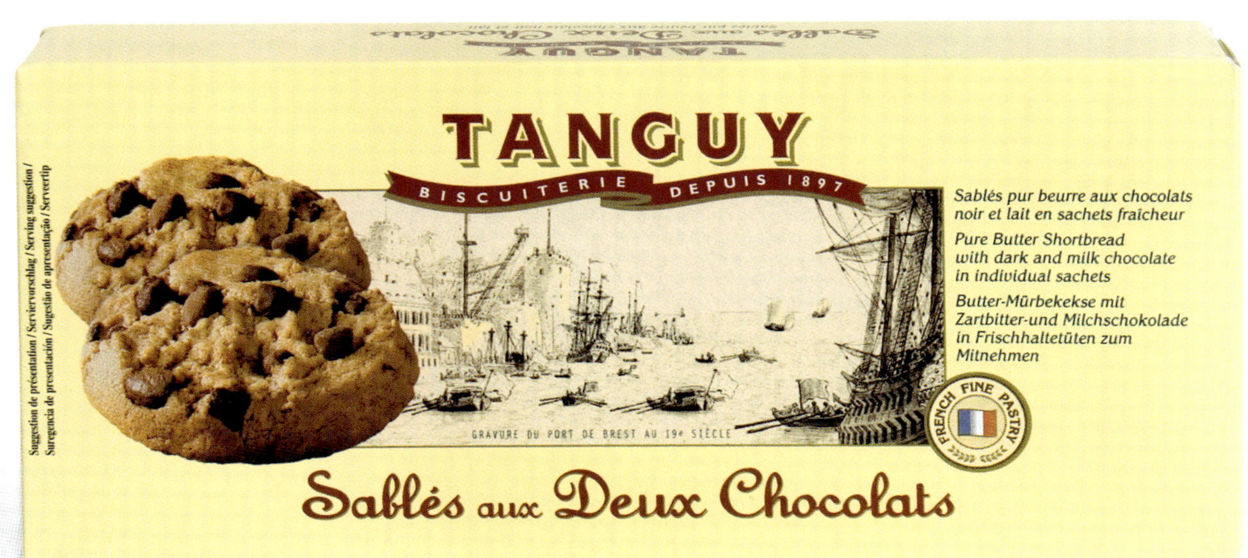

Suggestion de présentation / Servicevorschlag / Serving suggestion /
Surgerencia de presentación / Sugestão de apresentação / Serveertip

TANGUY
BISCUITERIE DEPUIS 1897

GRAVURE DU PORT DE BREST AU 19ᵉ SIÈCLE

Sablés pur beurre aux chocolats
noir et lait en sachets fraîcheur

Pure Butter Shortbread
with dark and milk chocolate
in individual sachets

Butter-Mürbekekse mit
Zartbitter- und Milchschokolade
in Frischhaltetüten zum
Mitnehmen

FRENCH FINE PASTRY

Sablés aux Deux Chocolats

tion dazu, lernen immer mehr Menschen, was TIONY ist, und ein solcher Name hat dann die Voraussetzung, ein »großer« Name zu werden.

Ein großer und bekannter Name kann viel, er kann aber nicht alles. So könnte man ja mit Glück auch den Familiennamen FERRARI tragen und überlegen, selbst eine Autofabrik oder eine Schmuckkollektion unter diesem Namen zu verkaufen. Doch genau hier gibt es die Grenzen. Sogenannte »berühmte« Marken sind Namen, die dem überwiegenden Teil der Menschen bekannt sind und damit auch den Ruf eines überragenden Schutzguts darstellen. Sie stehen also unter einem besonderen Schutz, da sie ja über lange Zeit und mit außergewöhnlich hohen Investitionen aufgebaut wurden, und dieser Schutz geht weit über die relevante Warenklasse hinaus.

ever more people will learn what TIONY is. At this point, such a name has what it takes to become a famous name.

Great and famous names can do a lot, but they can't do everything. For instance, one might be fortunate enough to share the family name FERRARI, and consider selling a car or a line of jewelry under the same name. But precisely here, there are restrictions. So-called "famous" brands are names that are known by a majority of people. Owing to this status, they enjoy special trademark protections that are legally grounded in the considerable investments and long periods of time it is likely to have taken to establish such a status. The trademark protection also tends to go well beyond the relevant product classification.

van Gogh Aquarellfarben, 2007
Farbkasten
2,5 x 13 x 10 cm (geöffnet: 20,5 cm)

van Gogh Watercolours, 2007.
Paint set
2.5 x 13 x 10 cm (open: 20.5 cm)

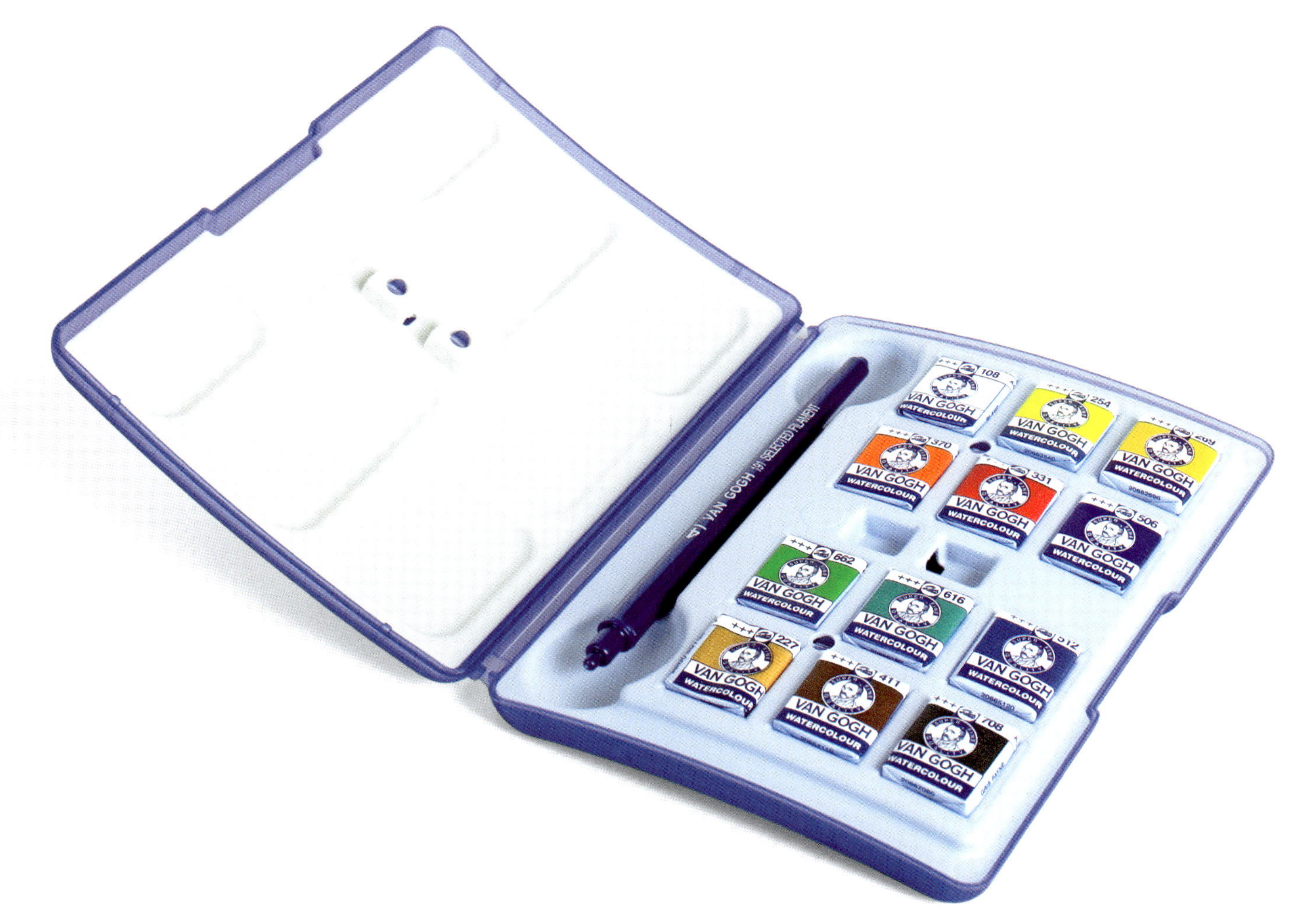

Wenn man also selbst einen solchen berühmten Namen trägt, sollte man sich vor der gewerblichen Nutzung von einem Fachmann beraten lassen, bevor man hinterher vor großen juristischen Problemen steht. Der Reiz, sich großer Namen zu bedienen ist natürlich groß, dafür sind sie zu verführerisch. Aber sie können natürlich auch das Gegenteil von dem bewirken, was man möchte. Namen sind eben nicht nur Schall und Rauch, wie Goethe meinte. ∎

Those who bear such famous names should therefore seek the advice of an expert before attempting to use them for commercial purposes. They otherwise might find themselves confronted by some of the world's highest paid lawyers. While the incentive for using famous names is clear enough, actually doing so may lead to the opposite of what one had hoped. Contrary to what Goethe once suggested, names are more than just hollow words. ∎

Vermeer BC2000XL, 2007
Holzhäcksler
330 x 437 x 250 cm

Vermeer BC2000XL, 2007
Brush chipperr
330 x 437 x 250 cm

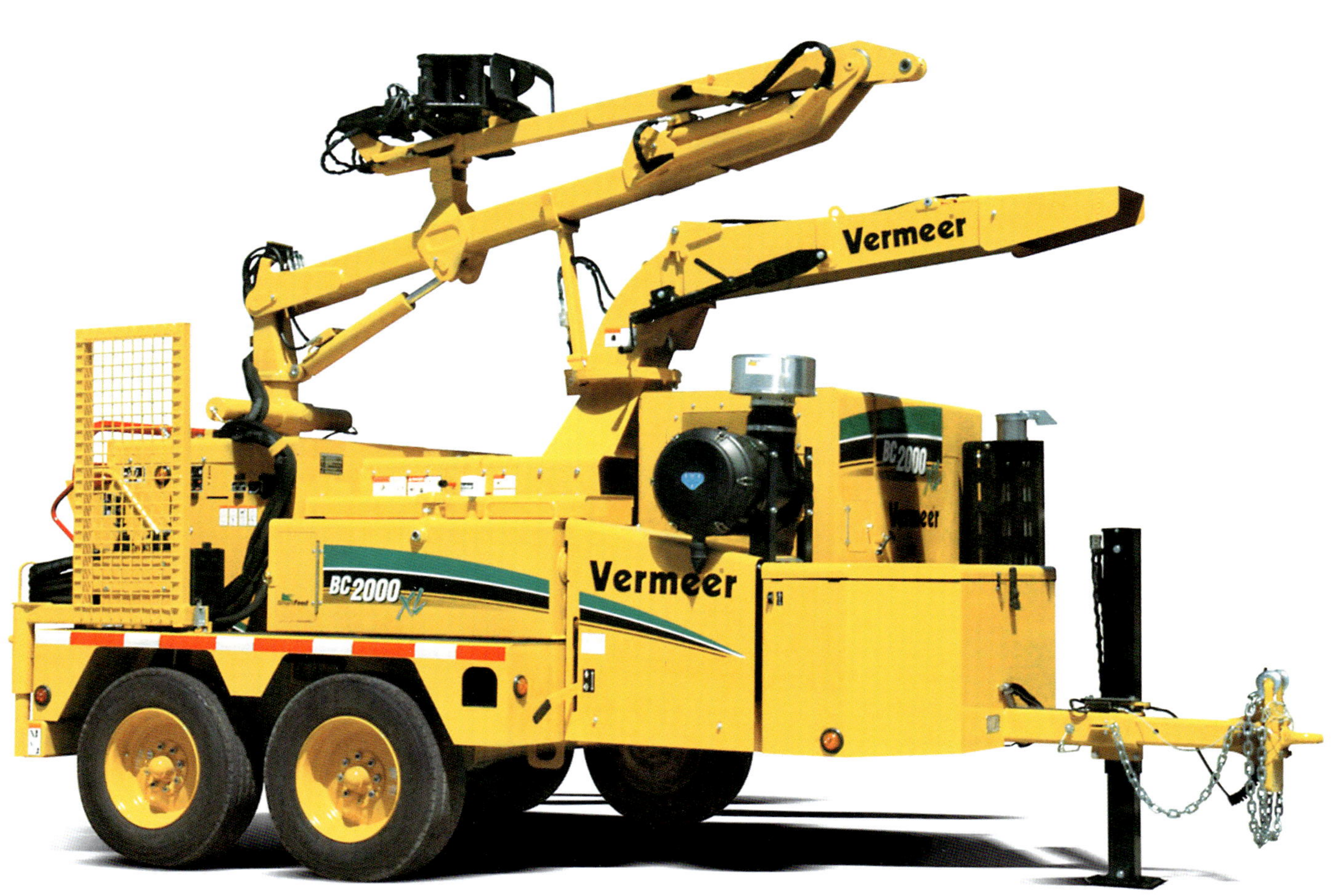

Vermeer
BC 2000 XL
BC 2000
Vermeer

Viola Olio extra vergine di oliva, 2007
Natives Olivenöl Extra
drei Flaschen à 0,75 l, Verpackung 40 x 26,6 x 9 cm

Viola Olio extra vergine di oliva, 2007
Extra virgin olive oil
three 0.75-liter bottles, package size: 40 x 26,6 x 9 cm

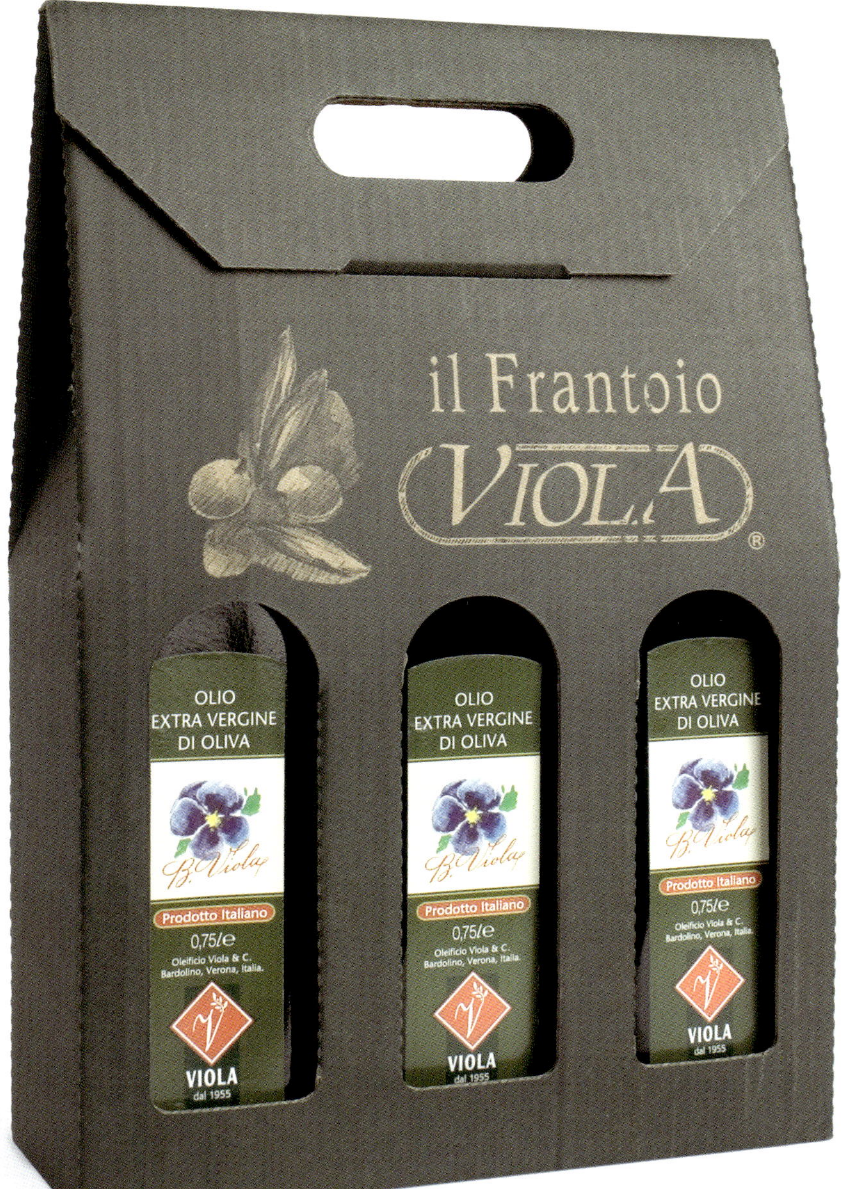
il Frantoio
VIOLA
OLIO
EXTRA VERGINE
DI OLIVA
B. Viola
Prodotto Italiano
0,75/ℓ
Oleificio Viola & C.
Bardolino, Verona, Italia.
VIOLA
dal 1955
OLIO
EXTRA VERGINE
DI OLIVA
B. Viola
Prodotto Italiano
0,75/ℓ
Oleificio Viola & C.
Bardolino, Verona, Italia.
VIOLA
dal 1955
OLIO
EXTRA VERGINE
DI OLIVA
B. Viola
Prodotto Italiano
0,75/ℓ
Oleificio Viola & C.
Bardolino, Verona, Italia.
VIOLA
dal 1955

Walther P99, 2005

Soft-Air-Pistole, Kaliber 6 mm

13 x 17,8 x 3 cm

Walther P99, 2005

6-mm airsoft pistol

13 x 17.8 x 3 cm

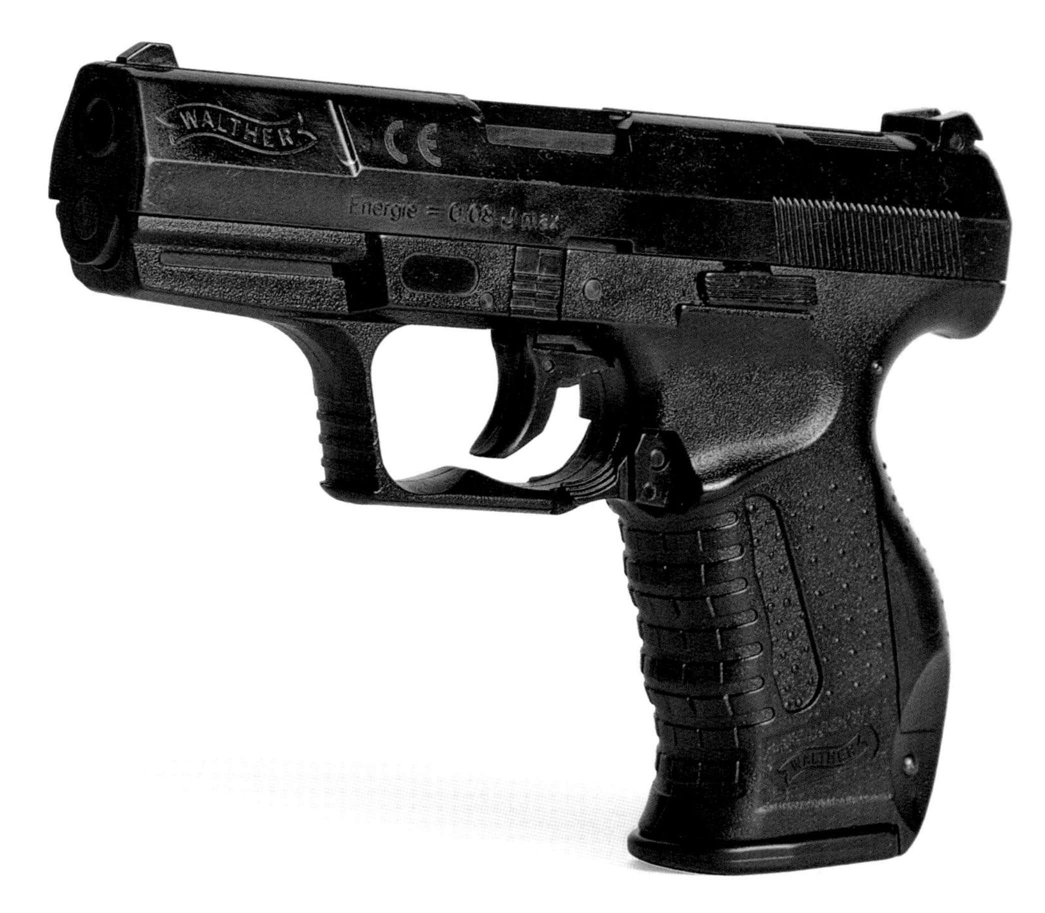

Produzenten und Künstler | Manufacturers and Artists

Appel Cicero, 2000
Sardinen, 125 g
2,7 x 10,7 x 6,3 cm
Appel Feinkost GmbH, Cuxhaven,
Deutschland

Karel Appel
1921 Amsterdam – 2006 Zürich
Niederländischer Maler in der Nachfolge
des Expressionismus, Mitbegründer der
internationalen Künstlergruppe Cobra

Appel Cicero, 2000
Sardines, 125 g / 2.7 x 10.7 x 6.3 cm
Appel Feinkost GmbH, Cuxhaven,
Germany

Karel Appel
1921 Amsterdam – 2006 Zurich
Dutch painter of the post World War
II era, co-founder of the international
CoBrA group

Bayer Aspirin N2, 2007
20 Tabletten
Schachtel 1,7 x 8,9 x 4 cm
Bayer Vital, Leverkusen,
Deutschland

Herbert Bayer
1900 Haag am Hausruck, Öster-
reich – 1985 Montecito, USA
Österreichischer Grafikdesigner,
Architekt, Maler und Fotograf, Lehrer am
Bauhaus

Bayer Aspirin N2, 2007
20 tablets / box size: 1.7 x 8.9 x 4 cm
Bayer Vital, Leverkusen, Germany

Herbert Bayer
1900 Haag am Hausruck, Österreich /
Austria – 1985 Montecito, USA
Austrian graphic artist, architect,
painter, and photographer, teacher at
the Bauhaus school

Dr. Beckmann Anti-Grau, 2005
Waschmittel
13,3 x 11,2 x 3,1 cm
delta pronatura Dr. Krauss &
Dr. Beckmann KG, Egelsbach,
Deutschland / Wien, Österreich

Max Beckmann
1884 Leipzig – 1950 New York
Deutscher Maler und Grafiker des
Expressionismus

Dr. Beckmann Anti-Gray, 2005
Detergent
13.3 x 11.2 x 3.1 cm
delta pronatura Dr. Krauss &
Dr. Beckmann KG, Egelsbach, Ger-
many/ Vienna, Austria

Max Beckmann
1884 Leipzig – 1950 New York
German expressionist painter and
graphic artist

Bellini, Il Cocktail di Venezia,
2000
0,75 l Flasche
Höhe 32,5 cm, ⌀ 8,5 cm
Canella Casa Vinicola s.p.a., San
Dona' di Piave (Venezia), Italien

Giovanni Bellini
um 1430 Venedig – 1516 Venedig
Venezianischer Maler, Schüler seines
Vaters Jacopo Bellini, Begründer der
oberitalienischen Frührenaissance mit
seinem Bruder Gentile Bellini

Bellini, The Venetian Cocktail,
2000
0.75 l bottle
height: 32.5 cm, ⌀ 8.5 cm
Canella Casa Vinicola s.p.a.,
San Dona' di Piave (Venice), Italy

Giovanni Bellini
c. 1430 Venice – 1516 Venice
Venetian painter, pupil of his father
Jacopo Bellini, founder of the Upper
Italian early renaissance together with
his brother Gentile Bellini

Beuys Dog Mix, 2005
Hundefutter, 20 kg
80 x 54 x 25 cm
Grünes Warenhaus Hugo Beuys,
Bedburg-Hau, Deutschland

Joseph Beuys
1921 Krefeld – 1986 Düsseldorf
Deutscher Plastiker, Zeichner, Aktions-
künstler, Kunsttheoretiker, Politiker und
Pädagoge, Erfinder der Sozialen Plastik

Beuys Dog Mix, 2005
Dog food, 20 kg
80 x 54 x 25 cm
Grünes Warenhaus Hugo Beuys,
Bedburg-Hau, Germany

Joseph Beuys
1921 Krefeld – 1986 Düsseldorf
German sculptor, draftsman, performance artist, art theoretician, politician,
and teacher, inventor of social sculpture

Breuer Comforta, 2007
Runddusche
190 x 100 x 100 cm
Horst Breuer GmbH & Co. KG,
Neuwied, Deutschland

Marcel Breuer
1902 Fünfkirchen, Ungarn –
1981 New York
Österreichisch-ungarischer Architekt und
Designer, Lehrer am Bauhaus

Breuer Comforta, 2007
Round shower
190 x 100 x 100 cm
Horst Breuer GmbH & Co. KG,
Neuwied, Germany

Marcel Breuer
1902 Fünfkirchen, Hungary – 1981
New York
Austrian-Hungarian architect and
designer, teacher at the Bauhaus school

Canaletto / Caravaggio /
Donatello, 2006
Steuergeräte für die Physiotherapie
aus der Serie Grandi maestri
Iontophoresis / Interferenz-
Elektrotherapie / Ultraschall-Therapie,
je 38 x 25 x 23 cm
LED s.p.a., Aprilia, Italien

Canaletto (Giovanni Antonio
Canal)
1697 Venedig – 1768 Venedig
Venezianischer Veduten- und Land-
schaftsmaler zur Zeit des Barock

Canaletto (Bernardo Bellotto)
um 1721/22 Venedig – 1780 Warschau
Venezianischer Vedutenmaler zur Zeit
des Barock, Neffe und Schüler des
Giovanni Antonio Canal

Caravaggio (Michelangelo Merisi
da Caravaggio)
1571 Mailand – 1610 Porto Ercole
Italienischer Künstler, Begründer der
römischen Barockmalerei

Donatello (Donato di Niccolò di
Betto Bardi)
1386 Florenz – 1466 Florenz
Italienischer Bildhauer, Begründer der
Frührenaissance in der Plastik

Canaletto / Caravaggio /
Donatello, 2006
Physical therapy control units from the
Grandi Maestri series
Iontophoresis / Interferential Therapy /
Ultrasound Therapy
(size of each unit: 38 x 25 x 23 cm)
LED s.p.a., Aprilia, Italy

Canaletto (Giovanni Antonio
Canal)
1697 Venice – 1768 Venice
Venetian town and landscape painter of
the baroque period

Canaletto (Bernardo Bellotto)
c. 1721/22 Venice – 1780 Warsaw
Venetian town and landscape painter of
the baroque period, nephew and pupil
of Giovanni Antonio Canal

Caravaggio (Michelangelo Merisi
da Caravaggio)
1571 Milan – 1610 Porto Ercole
Italian artist, founder of baroque Ro-
man painting

Donatello (Donato di Niccolò di
Betto Bardi)
1386 Florence – 1466 Florence
Italian sculptor, pioneer of early renaissance sculpture

Cellini Espressotasse, 2004
Tasse, Höhe 4,3 cm, ⌀ 5,3 cm
Untertasse, Höhe 1,3 cm, ⌀ 12 cm
Cellini s.p.a., Genua, Italien

Benvenuto Cellini
1500 Florenz – 1571 Florenz
Italienischer Goldschmied und Bildhauer
des Manierismus

Cellini Espresso Cup, 2004
Cup, height: 4.3 cm, ⌀ 5.3 cm
saucer, height: 1.3 cm, ⌀ 12 cm
Cellini s.p.a., Genoa, Italy

Benvenuto Cellini
1500 Florence – 1571 Florence
Italian goldsmith and sculptor of the
mannerist style

David Sonnenblumenkerne,
1998
106 g / 18,9 x 10,2 x 2,5 cm
Nestlé USA, Inc. – Sunmark Division,
David & Sons, Fresno, Kalifornien,
USA

Jacques-Louis David
1748 Paris – 1825 Brüssel
Französischer Maler der Revolutionszeit,
Begründer des Klassizismus

David Sunflower Seeds,
1998
106 g / 18.9 x 10.2 x 2.5 cm
Nestlé USA, Inc. – Sunmark Division,
David & Sons, Fresno, CA, USA

Jacques-Louis David
1748 Paris – 1825 Brussels
French painter of the revolution period,
pioneer of classicism

Dove Extra Sensitive, 1998
Feuchtigkeitscreme 0,2 l
12,5 x 9,2 x 3,9 cm
Unilever Deutschland GmbH,
Hamburg

Arthur Dove
1880 Canandaigua, New York –
1946 Huntington, New York
Amerikanischer Künstler, Begründer der
abstrakten Malerei in den USA

Dove Extra Sensitive, 1998
Moisturizing Cream
0.2 l / 12.5 x 9.2 x 3.9 cm
Unilever Deutschland GmbH, Hamburg, Germany

Arthur Dove
1880 Canandaigua, New York – 1946
Huntington, New York
American artist, founder of abstract
painting in the United States

Dreher, 2005
3 Bierflaschen à 0,33 l
20,5 x 18 x 6 cm
Heineken Italia s.p.a., Mailand, Italien

Peter Dreher
* 1932 Mannheim
Deutscher Maler konzeptionell
orientierter Bildserien

Duchamp, 2002
Syrah Wein, 1,5 l Magnum-Flasche
Höhe 35,5 cm, ø 10,8 cm
Duchamp Estate Winery, Healdsburg,
Kalifornien, USA

Marcel Duchamp
1887 Blainville-Crevon – 1968 Paris
Französischer Künstler, Begründer der
Objekt- und Konzeptkunst

Ernst, 2007
Katalysator / 9,5 x 104,1 x 20,5 cm
Ernst-Apparatebau GmbH & Co. KG,
Hagen, Deutschland

Max Ernst
1891 Brühl – 1976 Paris
Deutscher Maler, Grafiker und Plastiker
des Dada und des Surrealismus

Fini's Feinstes, 2007
Weizenmehl, 1000 g
15,5 x 12 x 7,3 cm.
Erste Wiener Walzmühle Vonmiller
GmbH, Schwechat, Österreich

Leonor Fini
1908 Buenos Aires – 1996 Paris
Argentinische Malerin des Surrealismus

Fontana Chymos Anana, 2004
Ananas-Saft 1 l
19,9 x 10,3 x 6,5 cm
New Sevegep Ltd., Nicosia,
Zypern

Lucio Fontana
1899 Rosario, Argentinien –
1968 Comabbio, Varese, Italien
Italienischer Maler, Begründer des
Spazialismo

Fragonard, 2007
Rosenseife / 3 x 8,8 x 5,9 cm
Fragonard Parfumeur, Grasse,
Frankreich

Jean-Honoré Fragonard
1732 Grasse – 1806 Paris
Französischer Maler und Grafiker des
Rokoko

Fuchs Fisch Würzer, 1999
80 g / Höhe 12 cm, ø 4,3 cm
Fuchs Gewürze GmbH, Dissen,
Deutschland

Ernst Fuchs
* 1930 Wien
Österreichischer Maler, Mitbegründer
der Wiener Schule des Phantastischen
Realismus

Giotto Stick, 2005
Klebestift / Höhe 10,1 cm, ø 2,6 cm
FILA, Fabbrica Italiana Lapis e Affini,
Pero (Mailand), Italien

Giotto di Bondone
1266 Colle di Vespignano –
1337 Florenz
Italienischer Maler und Architekt,
Wegbereiter der Renaissance

Dreher, 2005
Three 0.33-liter bottles of beer
20.5 x 18 x 6 cm
Heineken Italia s.p.a., Milan, Italy

Peter Dreher
* 1932 Mannheim
German painter of concept-oriented
image series

Duchamp, 2002
Syrah wine, magnum bottle
height: 35.5 cm, ø 10.8 cm
Duchamp Estate Winery, Healdsburg,
CA, USA

Marcel Duchamp
1887 Blainville-Crevon – 1968 Paris
French artist, inventor of object sculpture and concept art

Ernst, 2007
Catalytic converter
9.5 x 104.1 x 20.5 cm
Ernst-Apparatebau GmbH & Co. KG,
Hagen, Germany

Max Ernst
1891 Brühl – 1976 Paris
German painter, graphic artist, and
sculptor of the dada and surrealist style

Fini's Finest, 2007
Wheat flour, 1000 g
15.5 x 12 x 7.3 cm.
Erste Wiener Walzmühle Vonmiller
GmbH, Schwechat, Austria

Leonor Fini
1908 Buenos Aires – 1996 Paris
Argentine painter of the surrealist style

Fontana Chymos Anana, 2004
Pineapple juice, 1 l
19.9 x 10.3 x 6.5 cm
New Sevegep Ltd., Nicosia,
Cyprus

Lucio Fontana
1899 Rosario, Argentina –
1968 Comabbio, Varese, Italy
Italian painter, founder of spazialismo

Fragonard, 2007
Rose soap / 3 x 8.8 x 5.9 cm
Fragonard Parfumeur, Grasse,
France

Jean-Honoré Fragonard
1732 Grasse – 1806 Paris
French painter and graphic artist of the
rococo period

Fuchs Fish Spice, 1999
80 g / height: 12 cm, ø 4.3 cm
Fuchs Gewürze GmbH, Dissen,
Germany

Ernst Fuchs
* 1930 Vienna
Austrian painter, co-founder of the
Viennese school of phantastic realism

Giotto Stick, 2005
Glue stick / height: 10.1 cm, ø 2,6 cm
FILA, Fabbrica Italiana Lapis e Affini,
Pero (Milan), Italy

Giotto di Bondone
1266 Colle di Vespignano –
1337 Florence
Italian painter and architect, precursor
of the renaissance style

Goya Wiener Würstchen, 1998
142 g / Höhe 6,2 cm, ø 6,3 cm.
Goya Foods, Inc., Secaucus, New
Jersey, USA

Francisco de Goya
1746 Fuendetodos, Aragón —
1828 Bordeaux
Spanischer Hofmaler und gesellschafts-
kritischer Grafiker, Pionier der Aquatinta-
Radierung

Goya Vienna Sausage, 1998
142 g / height: 6.2 cm, ø 6.3 cm.
Goya Foods, Inc., Secaucus, NJ, USA

Francisco de Goya
1746 Fuendetodos, Aragón —
1828 Bordeaux
Spanish court painter, social critic and
graphic artist, pioneer of the aquatint
technique

Horn Brautkleid, 1968
Japanischer Stil / Größe 38
Horn Brautmode München GmbH,
München, Deutschland

Rebecca Horn
* 1944 Michelstadt
Deutsche Aktionskünstlerin und kineti-
sche Plastikerin

Roni Horn
* 1955 New York
Amerikanische Konzeptkünstlerin

Horn Wedding Dress, 1968
Japanese style / size 8
Horn Brautmode München GmbH,
Munich, Germany

Rebecca Horn
* 1944 Michelstadt
German performance artist and kinetic
sculptor

Roni Horn
* 1955 New York
American concept artist

Kandinsky Premiums &
Promotions, 2007
Schlüsselanhänger / 1 x 9,4 x 2,8 cm
Kandinsky Market Leading
Merchandise GmbH, Düsseldorf,
Deutschland

Wassily Kandinsky
1866 Moskau — 1944 Neuilly-sur-Seine,
Frankreich
Russischer Maler, Pionier der abstrakten
Malerei, Mitbegründer der Künstlergrup-
pe Der Blaue Reiter

Kandinsky Premiums &
Promotions, 2007
Key chain / 1 x 9.4 x 2,8 cm
Kandinsky Market Leading
Merchandise GmbH, Düsseldorf,
Germany

Wassily Kandinsky
1866 Moscow — 1944 Neuilly-sur-Seine,
France
Russian painter, pioneer of abstract
painting, co-founder of Der Blaue Reiter
group

Kauffmann Pikantes Allerlei,
2001
Feinsaures Essiggemüse, 670 g
Höhe 13,7 cm, ø 9,6 cm
Kauffmann GmbH & Co., Ebersbach/
Fils, Deutschland

Angelika Kauffmann
1741 Chur — 1807 Rom
Schweizer Porträtmalerin im Übergang
vom Rokoko zum Klassizismus

Kauffmann Pikantes Allerlei,
2001
Pickled vegetables, 670 g
height: 13.7 cm, ø 9.6 cm
Kauffmann GmbH & Co., Ebersbach/
Fils, Germany

Angelika Kauffmann
1741 Chur, Switzerland — 1807 Rome
Swiss portrait artist of the period
between rococo and classicism

Kiefer Roggenmischbrot, 2007
500 g, / ca. 20 x 18 x 12 cm
Kiefer Beck, Friesenheim, Deutschland

Anselm Kiefer
* 1945 Donaueschingen
Deutscher Plastiker und Maler ge-
schichtsorientierter, mythologischer Bilder

Kiefer Mixed Rye Bread, 2007
500 g, / 20 x 18 x 12 cm
Kiefer Beck, Friesenheim, Germany

Anselm Kiefer
* 1945 Donaueschingen
German sculptor and painter of historical, mythological images

Klein Q-ELITE XV, 2008
Rennrad, Spezialanfertigung mit
Karbonrahmen in International Klein
ca. 100 x 45 x 166 cm
Blue. Trek Bicycle Corp., Waterloo,
Wisconsin, USA

Yves Klein
1928 Nizza — 1962 Paris
Französischer Maler und Plastiker, Mitbegründer des Nouveau réalisme

Klein Q-ELITE XV, 2008
Custom racing bike with carbon frame
in International Klein Blue
c. 100 x 45 x 166 cm
Trek Bicycle Corp., Waterloo, WI, USA

Yves Klein
1928 Nice — 1962 Paris
French painter and sculptor, co-founder
of nouveau réalisme

Leonardo Transparente, 2004
60 m Klebeband /
Verpackung 16,1 x 11,6 x 2 cm
Syrom '90 s.p.a., Vinci (Florenz),
Italien

Leonardo da Vinci
1452 Anchiano, Vinci — 1519 Clos Lucé,
Amboise
Maler, Bildhauer, Architekt und Erfinder,
Universalgenie der italienischen Hochre-
naissance

Leonardo Transparente, 2004
60 m roll of tape
package size: 16.1 x 11.6 x 2 cm
Syrom '90 s.p.a., Vinci (Florence), Italy

Leonardo da Vinci
1452 Anchiano, Vinci, Italy — 1519 Clos
Lucé, Amboise, France
Painter, sculptor, architect, and inventor,
universal genius of the Italian renaissance

Lichtenstein Vitamin B 12, 2007
1 ml Injektionslösung
Höhe 4,8 cm, ⌀ 1,1 cm.
Winthrop Arzneimittel GmbH, Fürstenfeldbruck, Deutschland

Roy Lichtenstein
1923 New York – 1997 New York
Amerikanischer Maler von Comic-Motiven, Hauptvertreter der Pop Art

Lichtenstein Vitamin B 12, 2007
Injection solution, 1 ml
height: 4.8 cm, ⌀ 1.1 cm
Winthrop Arzneimittel GmbH, Fürstenfeldbruck, Germany

Roy Lichtenstein
1923 New York – 1997 New York
American painter of comic-strip subjects, major exponent of pop art

Lotto Go Centrale 2000
Fußballschuhe / Größe 42,
je 13 x 28 x 9,8 cm.
Lotto Sport Italia s.p.a., Trevignano (Treviso), Italien

Lorenzo Lotto
1480 Venedig – 1557 Loreto
Italienischer Maler zwischen Renaissance und Manierismus

Lotto Go Centrale 2000
Football shoes / size 8.5
13 x 28 x 9.8 cm
Lotto Sport Italia s.p.a., Trevignano (Treviso), Italy

Lorenzo Lotto
1480 Venedig – 1557 Loreto
Italian painter of the period between renaissance and mannerism

Manet S 100, 1960
Motorroller / 150 x 196 x 56,5 cm
Fahrzeugfabrik Považské strojárne n.p., Považskà Bystrica, CSSR

Édouard Manet
1832 Paris – 1883 Paris
Französischer Maler im Übergang vom Realismus zum Impressionismus

Manet S 100, 1960
Scooter / 150 x 196 x 56.5 cm
Vehicle factory Považské strojárne n.p., Považskà Bystrica, CSSR

Édouard Manet
1832 Paris – 1883 Paris
French painter of the period between realism and impressionism

Martini bianco, 2005
Wermut, 1 l / 32,1 x 8,8 x 7,5 cm
Martini & Rossi s.p.a., Turin, Italien

Simone Martini
1284 Siena – 1344 Avignon
Sienesischer Maler, Mitbegründer des Internationalen gotischen Stils

Martini Bianco, 2005
Vermouth, 1 l / 32.1 x 8.8 x 7.5 cm
Martini & Rossi s.p.a., Torino, Italy

Simone Martini
1284 Siena – 1344 Avignon
Sienese painter, co-founder of the international gothic style

Merz Spezial Dragees, 1999
60 Tabletten
Verpackung 9,8 x 5,2 x 3,8 cm
Merz Pharma GmbH & Co. KGaA, Frankfurt/Main, Deutschland

Mario Merz
1925 Mailand – 2003 Turin
Italienischer Mediziner und Plastiker der Arte povera

Gerhard Merz
* 1947 Mammendorf, München
Deutscher Maler, Gestalter architektonischer Farbräume

Merz Special Dragées, 1999
60 tablets
package size: 9.8 x 5.2 x 3.8 cm
Merz Pharma GmbH & Co. KGaA, Frankfurt, Germany

Mario Merz
1925 Milan – 2003 Torino
Italian physician and sculptor of Arte povera

Gerhard Merz
* 1947 Mammendorf/Munich
German painter, designer of architectural color spaces

Michelangelo superscharf, 2005
Brotmesser / 1 x 1,9 x 21,3 cm
Michelin Besteck- und Metallwarenfabrik GmbH, Krefeld, Deutschland

Michelangelo Buonarroti
1475 Caprese – 1564 Rom
Italienischer Bildhauer, Maler, Architekt und Dichter, Hauptvertreter der Renaissance, Begründer des Manierismus

Michelangelo super sharp, 2005
Bread knife / 1 x 1.9 x 21.3 cm
Michelin Besteck- und Metallwarenfabrik GmbH, Krefeld, Germany

Michelangelo Buonarroti
1475 Caprese – 1564 Rome
Italian sculptor, painter, architect, poet, and major exponent of the renaissance, founder of mannerism

Miro Femme, 2007
Eau de Parfum, 0,075 l
10,9 x 8,4 x 3,1 cm
Createurs Cosmetiques, Maxim Markenprodukte, Pulheim/Brauweiler, Deutschland

Joan Miró
1893 Mont-Roig del Camp – 1983 Palma de Mallorca
Katalanischer Maler, Grafiker und Bildhauer des Surrealismus

Miro Femme, 2007
Eau de perfume, 0,075 l
10.9 x 8.4 x 3.1 cm
Createurs Cosmetiques, Maxim Markenprodukte, Pulheim/Brauweiler, Germany

Joan Miró
1893 Mont-Roig del Camp – 1983 Palma de Mallorca
Catalonian painter, graphic artist, and sculptor of surrealism

Monet-Goyon AL5, 1936
Motorrad 500 ccm
ca. 80 x 200 x 80 cm
Joseph Monet & Adrien Goyon,
Macon, Frankreich

Claude Monet
1840 Paris – 1926 Giverny
Französischer Maler, Mitbegründer und
Hauptvertreter des Impressionismus

Monet-Goyon AL5, 1936
Motorcycle 500 ccm
80 x 200 x 80 cm
Joseph Monet & Adrien Goyon,
Macon, France

Claude Monet
1840 Paris – 1926 Giverny
French painter, co-founder and major
exponent of impressionism

Mueller's Dünne Spaghetti,
1998
227 g / 5,5 x 2,6 x 25,8 cm
CPC International Inc., Englewood
Cliffs, New Jersey, USA

Otto Mueller
1874 Liebau –
1930 Obernigk bei Breslau
Deutscher Maler und Grafiker, Mitglied
der expressionistischen Künstlergruppe
Brücke

Mueller's Thin Spaghetti, 1998
227 g / 5.5 x 2.6 x 25.8 cm
CPC International Inc., Englewood
Cliffs, New Jersey, USA

Otto Mueller
1874 Liebau – 1930 Obernigk bei
Breslau, Silesia
German painter and graphic artist,
member of the expressionist Brücke
group

Newman's Own, 2000
Venezianische Spaghettisauce mit
Pilzen, 737 g
Höhe 16,7 cm, ⌀ 8,9 cm
Newman's Own, Westport, Connec-
ticut, USA

Barnett Newman
1905 New York – 1970 New York
Amerikanischer Künstler, Pionier des
Color Field Painting

Newman's Own, 2000
Venetian Spaghetti Sauce with Mushrooms, 737 g
height: 16.7 cm, ⌀ 8.9 cm
Newman's Own, Westport, CT, USA

Barnett Newman
1905 New York – 1970 New York
American artist, pioneer of color field
painting

Citroën C4 Picasso, 2007
Kombilimousine
161-166,5 x 446,8 x 183,1 cm
PSA Peugeot Citroën,
Vigo Pontevedra, Spanien

Pablo Ruiz Picasso
1881 Málaga –
1973 Mougins, Frankreich
Spanischer Maler, Grafiker und Bildhauer,
Mitbegründer des Kubismus

Citroën C4 Picasso, 2007
Minivan
161-166.5 x 446.8 x 183.1 cm
PSA Peugeot Citroën, Vigo Pontevedra,
Spain

Pablo Ruiz Picasso
1881 Málaga, Spain – 1973 Mougins,
France
Spanish painter, graphic artist, and
sculptor, co-founder of cubism

Raffaello, 2007
Kokos-Mandel-Konfekt, 230 g
19 x 14 x 9,5 cm
Ferrero Deutschland GmbH, Frankfurt/
Main, Deutschland

Raffael (Raffaello da Urbino,
Raffaello Santi, Raffaello Sanzio)
1483 Urbino – 1520 Rom
Italienischer Maler und Baumeister,
Hauptvertreter der Renaissance

Raffaello, 2007
Coconut almond confectionery, 230 g
19 x 14 x 9.5 cm
Ferrero Deutschland GmbH, Frankfurt/
Main, Germany

Raffael
(Raffaello da Urbino, Raffaello Santi,
Raffaello Sanzio) 1483 Urbino –
1520 Rome
Italian painter and architect, major
exponent of the renaissance

Rauch SU602, 2007
Winterdienststreuer
142 x 132 x 220 cm
Rauch Landmaschinenfabrik GmbH,
Sinzheim, Deutschland

Christian Daniel Rauch
1777 Arolsen – 1857 Dresden
Bildhauer des Klassizismus

Neo Rauch
* 1960 Leipzig
Deutscher Maler, Hauptvertreter der
Neuen Leipziger Schule

Rauch SU602, 2007
Gritter / 142 x 132 x 220 cm
Rauch Landmaschinenfabrik GmbH,
Sinzheim, Germany

Christian Daniel Rauch
1777 Arolsen – 1857 Dresden
Bildhauer des Klassizismus

Neo Rauch
* 1960 Leipzig
German painter, major exponent of the
new Leipzig school

Rembrandt, 1997
Zahnpasta, 85 g / 6,5 x 17,6 x 2,9 cm
Den-Mat Corporation, Santa Maria,
California, USA

Rembrandt Harmensz van Rijn
1606 Leiden – 1669 Amsterdam
Holländischer Maler und Grafiker, Hauptvertreter des Barock

Rembrandt, 1997
Toothpaste, 85 g / 6.5 x 17.6 x 2.9 cm
Den-Mat Corporation, Santa Maria,
CA, USA

Rembrandt Harmensz van Rijn
1606 Leiden – 1669 Amsterdam
Dutch painter and graphic artist, major
exponent of the baroque style

Richter Feuer-Röllchen, 2001
Heringsfilets, 120 g
Höhe 4,3 cm, ø 10,1 cm
Richter & Greif Feinkost, Cuxhaven,
Deutschland

Adrian Ludwig Richter
1803 Dresden – 1884 Loschwitz /
Dresden
Deutscher Illustrator und Maler zwischen
Romantik und Biedermeier

Gerhard Richter
*1932 Dresden
Deutscher Maler mit Werkgruppen von
der Pop Art über den Fotorealismus bis
zur abstrakten Kunst

Richter Fire Rolls, 2001
Herring fillets, 120 g
height: 4.3 cm, ø 10.1 cm
Richter & Greif Feinkost, Cuxhaven,
Germany

Adrian Ludwig Richter
1803 Dresden – 1884 Loschwitz /
Dresden
German illustrator and painter of the
period between the romantic and
Biedermeier periods

Gerhard Richter
*1932 Dresden
German painter who created disparate
works from pop art to photo realism
and abstract art

Rietveld, 2000
T-Shirt (Rückseite) / Größe M
Fortune Fashions, Los Angeles,
Kalifornien, USA

Gerrit Rietveld
1888 Utrecht – 1964 Utrecht
Niederländischer Architekt und Designer,
Mitglied der Künstlergruppe De Stijl

Rietveld, 2000
T-shirt (back) / size M
Fortune Fashions, Los Angeles, CA,
USA

Gerrit Rietveld
1888 Utrecht – 1964 Utrecht
Dutch architect and designer, member
of the De Stijl group

Schick Slim Twin ST, 1998
5 Nassrasierer
Verpackung 12,4 x 12,6 x 2 cm
Warner-Lambert Co. Shaving Products
Group, Milford, Connecticut, USA

Christian Gottlieb Schick
1776 Stuttgart – 1812 Stuttgart
Deutscher Maler des Klassizismus mit
Tendenz zur Romantik

Schick Slim Twin ST, 1998
5 razors / package size: 12.4 x 12.6
x 2 cm
Warner-Lambert Co. Shaving Products
Group, Milford, CT, USA

Christian Gottlieb Schick
1776 Stuttgart – 1812 Stu+ttgart
German painter of the classicist period
with a tendency towards the romantic
style

Sierra bali, 2005
Strandmuschel,
offen 120 x 250 x 110 cm
verpackt ca. 62 cm, ø 13 cm
Intersport Deutschland EG

Santiago Sierra
* 1966 Madrid
Spanischer Konzeptkünstler gesell-
schaftskritischer Projekte

Sierra bali, 2006
Beach tent, open: 120 x 250 x 110 cm
packed: 62 cm, ø 13 cm
Intersport Germany EG

Santiago Sierra
* 1966 Madrid
Spanish concept artist and social critic

Sisley, 2007
Damenschuhe Größe 37 / je 6,9 x
24,8 x 8,4 cm
Bencom s.r.l., Ponzano Veneto
(Treviso), Italien

Alfred Sisley
1839 Paris – 1899 Moret-sur-Loing
Englisch-französischer Maler des
Impressionismus

Sisley, 2007
Women's shoes, size 6
6.9 x 24.8 x 8.4 cm
Bencom s.r.l., Ponzano Veneto
(Treviso), Italy

Alfred Sisley
1839 Paris – 1899 Moret-sur-Loing
English-French painter of the impres-
sionist style

Stella, 2005
Hartweizengrieß, 500 g
21,9 x 10,5 x 3,5 cm
Melissa Kikizas Food Products S.A.,
Athen, Griechenland

Jacques Stella
1596 Lyon – 1657 Paris
Französischer Maler und Grafiker des
Barock

Joseph Stella
1877 Muro Lucano, Italien –
1946 New York
Italienisch-amerikanischer Maler des
Futurismus

Frank Stella
* 1936 Malden, Massachusetts
Amerikanischer Maler und Plastiker,
Erfinder der Shaped Canvas

Stella, 2005
Durum wheat semolina, 500 g / 21.9 x
10.5 x 3.5 cm
Melissa Kikizas Food Products S.A.,
Athens, Greece

Jacques Stella
1596 Lyon – 1657 Paris
French painter and graphic artist of the
baroque age

Joseph Stella
1877 Muro Lucano, Italy –
1946 New York
Italian-American painter of futurism

Frank Stella
* 1936 Malden, Massachusetts
American painter and sculptor, exponent of the hard egde style, inventor of
the shaped canvas

Tanguy, Sablés pur beurre aux
deux chocolats, 2006
Butter-Mürbekeks mit zwei
Schokoladensorten, 150 g
9,8 x 27,5 x 3,7 cm
Fouesnant, Frankreich

Yves Tanguy
1900 Paris – 1955 Woodbury, USA
Französischer Maler surrealistischer
Landschaften

Tanguy Sablés pur beurre aux
deux chocolats, 2006
Shortbread with two sorts of
chocolate, 150 g
9.8 x 27.5 x 3.7 cm
Tanguy, Fouesnant, France

Yves Tanguy
1900 Paris – 1955 Woodbury, USA
French painter of surrealistic landscapes

van Gogh Aquarellfarben, 2007
Farbkasten / 2,5 x 13 x 10 cm
(geöffnet: 20,5 cm)
Royal Talens, Holland

Vincent van Gogh
1853 Groot-Zundert, Niederlande – 1890
Auvers-sur-Oise, Frankreich
Niederländischer Maler und Zeichner
des Realismus und Impressionismus,
Wegbereiter des Expressionismus

van Gogh Watercolour, 2007
Paint set / 2.5 x 13 x 10 cm
(open: 20.5 cm)
Royal Talens, The Netherlands

Vincent van Gogh
1853 Groot-Zundert, The Netherlands –
1890 Auvers-sur-Oise, France
Dutch painter and draftsman, pioneer of
expressionism

Vermeer BC2000XL, 2007
Trommelhäcksler
ca. 330 x 437 x 250 cm
Vermeer Manufacturing Company,
Pella, Iowa, USA

Jan Vermeer van Delft
getauft 1632 Delft – 1675 Delft
Holländischer Maler barocker Genresze-
nen und Interieurs

Vermeer BC2000XL, 2007
Brush chipper, 330 x 437 x 250 cm
Vermeer Manufacturing Company,
Pella, IA, USA

Jan Vermeer van Delft
baptized 1632 Delft – 1675 Delft
Dutch painter of baroque genre paintings and interiors

Viola Olio extra vergine di oliva,
2007
Natives Olivenöl Extra
3 Flaschen à 0,75 l
Verpackung 40 x 26,6 x 9 cm
Oleificio Viola & C., Bardolino
(Verona), Italien

Bill Viola
* 1951 New York
Amerikanischer Videokünstler

Viola Olio extra vergine di oliva,
2007
Extra virgin olive oil /
three 0.75-liter bottles,
package size: 40 x 26,6 x 9 cm
Oleificio Viola & C., Bardolino
(Verona), Italy

Bill Viola
* 1951 New York
American video artist who focused on
existential and religious topics

Walther P99, 2005
Soft-Air-Pistole, Kaliber 6 mm
13 x 17,8 x 3 cm
Umax Sportwaffen GmbH & Co. KG,
Arnsberg, Deutschland

Franz Erhard Walther
* 1939 Fulda
Deutscher Künstler, Begründer der Plastik
als Handlungsform

Walther P99, 2005
6-mm airsoft pistol / 13 x 17.8 x 3 cm
Umax Sportwaffen GmbH & Co. KG,
Arnsberg, Germany

Franz Erhard Walther
* 1939 Fulda
German artist, founder of interactive
sculpture

Dank | Acknowledgements

Für wertvollen Rat, Informationen und Unterstützung geht der herzliche Dank von Michael Klant an | For their valuable advice and generous support, Michael Klant would like to thank the following individuals: Andreas Bee, Petr Beer, Gerhard Birkhofer, Ulrich Birtel, Diffidato, Marcus Gesierich, Isabel Herda, Justus Kampp, Damaris Klant, Jochen Ludwig, Thomas Oswald, Nasser Parvizi, Raphael Spielmann, Timm Ulrichs, Josef Walch.

Alle Exponate gehören zur ArtBrands-Sammlung Klant, bis auf die folgenden, die dankenswerterweise von den Firmen ausgeliehen wurden | All exhibits belong to The Klant ArtBrands Collection, except for the ones that have been generously loaned by the following companies: Breuer, Duchamp, Ernst, Horn, Canaletto, Caravaggio, Donatello, Klein, Citroën Picasso, Rauch, Vermeer

Die Monet-Goyon AL5 wurde zur Verfügung gestellt von | The Monet-Goyon AL5 has been provided by Frank Brossette

Folgende Exponate sind Schenkungen | The following exhibits have been donated: Michelangelo von | by Herbert Wentscher
Tanguy von | by Thomas Heyl

Autorenverzeichnis | List of Authors

Dr. Angelika Epple, Historikerin. Akademische Rätin am Historischen Seminar der Albert-Ludwigs-Universität Freiburg. | Dr. Angelika Epple, historian. Lecturer at the History Department of the University of Freiburg.

Dr. Günter Figal, Philosoph. Professor am Philosophischen Seminar der Albert-Ludwigs-Universität Freiburg. | Dr. Günter Figal, philosopher. Professor at the Philosophy Department of the University of Freiburg.

Manfred Gotta, Spezialist für die Entwicklung neuer Namen für neue Produkte, Unternehmen und Dienstleistungen. Gotta Brands, Forbach, Deutschland. | Manfred Gotta, specialist in the development of new names for new products, companies, and services. Gotta Brands, Forbach, Germany.

Dr. Michael Klant, Künstler, Kunsthistoriker, Kunstlehrer. Professor am Institut der Künste, Pädagogische Hochschule Freiburg. | Dr. Michael Klant, artist, art historian, art teacher. Professor at the Art Department, University of Education Freiburg.

Dr. Jochen Ludwig, Kunsthistoriker. Direktor des Museums für Neue Kunst Freiburg. | Dr. Jochen Ludwig, art historian. Director of The Freiburg Museum of New Art.

Fotonachweis | Photo Credits

Firmenfotografien wurden freundlicherweise zur Verfügung gestellt von | Company photographs have been generously provided by Breuer, Canaletto, Caravaggio, Donatello, Klein, Picasso, Rauch, Vermeer

Manet-Foto von | Manet photograph by Jacqueline Zimmer

Ausleuchtung von | Lighting by Nasser Parvizi

Retuschen von | Retouching by Marcus Gesierich

© Fotografien | Photographs by Michael Klant

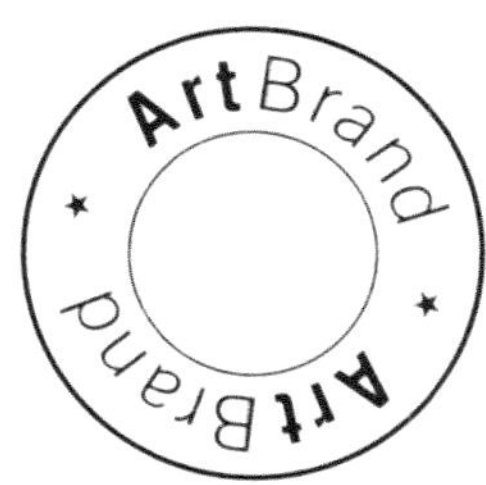

Impressum | Colophon

Diese Publikation erscheint anlässlich der Ausstellung | This catalogue is published in conjunction with the exhibition:

ArtBrands
wenn Hunde Beuys fressen | when dogs eat Beuys

Eine Sammlung von | a collection by Michael Klant

1. März – 4. Mai 2008 | March 1– May 4, 2008
Museum für Neue Kunst, Freiburg | The Freiburg Museum of New Art

Herausgeber | Editor: Städtische Museen Freiburg; Museum für Neue Kunst, Freiburg i. Br., Deutschland |
The Museums of the City of Freiburg; The Freiburg Museum of New Art, Germany

Redaktion | Editing: Jochen Ludwig, Michael Klant

Übersetzungen | Translations: Dennis Cole

Grafische Gestaltung und Satz | Graphic design and typesetting: Ulrich Birtel, Pädagogische Hochschule | University of Education Freiburg

Schrift | Typeface: Frutiger · Papier | Paper: BVS matt, 135 g/m²

Reproduktionen | Reproductions: Dr. Cantz'sche Druckerei

Druck und Buchbinderei | Printing and binding: fgb freiburger graphische betriebe

© 2008 Hatje Cantz Verlag, Ostfildern; Museum für Neue Kunst Freiburg; und Autoren | and authors

© 2008 für die abgebildeten Fotografien, mit Ausnahme der auf S. 119 erwähnten Fälle |
for the reproduced photographs, unless otherwise stated on p. 119: Michael Klant

© 2008 für die Umschlagabbildung | for the cover illustration: Getty Images

Erschienen im | Published by
Hatje Cantz Verlag · Zeppelinstrasse 32 · 73760 Ostfildern · Deutschland | Germany
Tel. +49 711 4405-200 · Fax +49 711 4405-220
www.hatjecantz.com

Hatje Cantz books are available internationally at selected bookstores.
For more information about our distribution partners please visit our homepage at www.hatjecantz.com.

ISBN 978-3-7757-2116-5

Printed in Germany

Dank an den Förderverein des Museums für Neue Kunst Freiburg mit seinen Partnern |
Thanks to the Friends of The Freiburg Museum of New Art and its partners

Duravit AG, Hornberg
Rhodia Acetow GmbH, Freiburg i. Br.
Sparwasser & Heilshorn Rechtsanwälte Partnerschaften, Freiburg i. Br.

Ausstellungstechnik und konservatorische Betreuung | Exhibition technique and conservation services:
Werkstätten der Städtischen Museen Freiburg, Restaurierungsabteilung des Augustinermuseums und des Museums für Neue Kunst |
Workshops of The Museums of the City of Freiburg, Restoration Department of The Augustinermuseum and of The Freiburg Museum of New Art

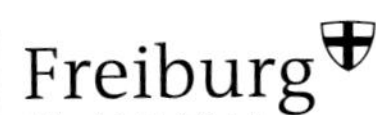

Museum für Neue Kunst Freiburg
Marienstrasse 10a · 79098 Freiburg · Deutschland | Germany
Tel. 0049-(0)761-201-2581 · Fax. 0049-(0)761-201-2589
www.freiburg.de/museen · mnk@stadt.freiburg.de